BRUCE NASH & ALLAN ZULLO'S
SPORTS
HALL OF SHA
GOLF
CARTOO
CLASSICS
THE MOST OUTRAGEOUS MOMENTS IN GOLF HISTORY!

TRIBUNE
PUBLISHING
Orlando/1993

# SPORTS HALL OF SHAME
## GOLF CARTOON CLASSICS



A publication of Tribune Publishing
and Tribune Media Services, Inc.


For information:
Tribune Publishing,
P.O. Box 1100, Orlando, Florida 32802

Printed in the United States
January 1993

ISBN 0-941263-76-2

# DEDICATION

To Steve Shepherd, a true champion
in every sense of the word.

— **Bruce Nash**

To Kay and Dwight Linquist, straight shooters in life –
but not necessarily on the golf course.

— **Allan Zullo**

To Dan and Judy, my two best shots ever.

— **Bill Maul**

# SHANKS FOR THE MEMORIES

In 1984, we began chronicling hilarious happenings and ignoble incidents in the world of sports in our *Sports Hall of Shame* book series. Six years later, we teamed up with comic illustrator Bill Maul and began producing the nationally syndicated *Sports Hall of Shame* cartoon feature to honor these outrageously funny but true moments in sports. In 1992, we compiled some of our favorites in *Sports Hall of Shame Cartoon Classics Vol. 1.*

Although every major sport is represented in *Cartoon Classics,* there's one sport that boasts such a rich heritage of shameful shenanigans that it deserves its own book – golf. So we've packed this book with our funniest cartoons of zany moments from tee to green. Like, for instance, the time when:

• At the 1938 U.S. Open, Ray Ainsley blasted his way to a record score of 19 – for one hole!

• Gary Player, in one of his first tournaments, got knocked out by his own ball!

• Hale Irwin blew the 1983 British Open by whiffing a three-inch putt!

Whether you're a par-birdie-par pro or a slice-your-drive, cut-your-Titleist weekend hacker, we hope you'll enjoy this light-hearted tribute to a centuries-old sport.

Meanwhile, we will continue to chronicle the embarrassing and funny moments in golf as they happen. We won't play favorites. We will turn our spotlight of shame on both the heroes and the zeroes. As our motto says, "Fame *and* shame are part of the game."

PLAYING A PRACTICE ROUND BEFORE THE 1967 MASTERS, CRAFTY VETERAN **SAM SNEAD** TOLD ROOKIE BOBBY COLE THAT WHEN HE WAS HIS AGE (20), HE COULD DRIVE HIS BALL OVER THE 50-FOOT-TALL PINE TREES LINING THE 13TH HOLE. TAKING THE CHALLENGE, COLE LIFTED A DRIVE TOWARD THE TREES — ONLY TO HAVE IT GOBBLED UP BY THE TOWERING PINES. *"MAN, I CAN'T HIT THE BALL OVER THOSE TREES. HOW DID YOU DO IT?"* ASKED COLE. THE 55-YEAR-OLD SNEAD SMILED AND SAID, *"WHEN I WAS YOUR AGE, THOSE TREES WERE ONLY 20 FEET TALL."*

AMONG THE MANY UNSETTLING LOCAL RULES AT THE **ELEPHANT HILLS COUNTRY CLUB** IN VICTORIA FALLS, ZIMBABWE, AFRICA:

• IF A BALL COMES TO REST WITHIN A TAIL'S DISTANCE OF A SLEEPING BUFFALO, IT MAY BE REMOVED AND DROPPED NO NEARER THE HOLE WITHOUT PENALTY. MORE THAN A TAIL'S LENGTH, THE BALL SHALL BE PLAYED AS IT LIES.

DURING A PRACTICE ROUND BEFORE THE 1970 MILLER OPEN, GOLFER JERRY McGEE WAS BENDING OVER TO TEE UP HIS BALL WHEN ONE OF HIS PLAYING PARTNERS, **BILL BLANTON**, TOOK A PRACTICE SWING. UNFORTUNATELY, BLANTON HAD HIS EYE ON THE BALL—AND NOT ON McGEE. THE SOLID BLOW TO THE HEAD KNOCKED McGEE OUT OF ACTION FOR SEVERAL WEEKS!

FORMER YALE FOOTBALL COACH **REGGIE ROOT** SMACKED FOUR STRAIGHT BALLS INTO A POND ON THE NINTH HOLE OF THE YALE UNIVERSITY GOLF COURSE. HE WALKED TO THE EDGE OF THE WATER WHERE HIS CADDIE ASKED, "*DO YOU WANT TO DROP A BALL?*" REPLIED ROOT:

I DO NOT. I WANT TO DROP MY BAG!

HE DID JUST THAT AND NEVER PLAYED GOLF AGAIN.

AT MIAMI'S DORAL COUNTRY CLUB IN 1965, SMALL, SLENDER GOLFER **CHI CHI RODRIGUEZ** TOLD A BIG, BURLY IRISHMAN, *"I'LL LET YOU HIT A DRIVE AND A WEDGE SHOT AND I'LL BET THAT YOU STILL WON'T BE ABLE TO CATCH UP TO MY DRIVE."* TAKING THE BET, THE IRISHMAN BELTED A MONSTROUS 320-YARD DRIVE—THEN REALIZED HE'D BEEN DUPED WHEN CHI CHI TURNED AROUND 180 DEGREES AND BLASTED HIS TEE SHOT IN THE OPPOSITE DIRECTION!

PRO GOLFER **ANDY BEAN** MADE AN EASY TWO-INCH TAP-IN AT THE 1983 CANADIAN OPEN THAT COST HIM A CHANCE TO WIN. HE TAPPED THE BALL IN WITH THE GRIP OF HIS PUTTER INSTEAD OF THE HEAD. ONLY THEN DID HE LEARN THAT HE HAD COMMITTED AN INFRACTION AND WAS ASSESSED A TWO-STROKE PENALTY. ANDY MISSED GETTING INTO THE PLAY-OFF BY THOSE TWO STROKES!

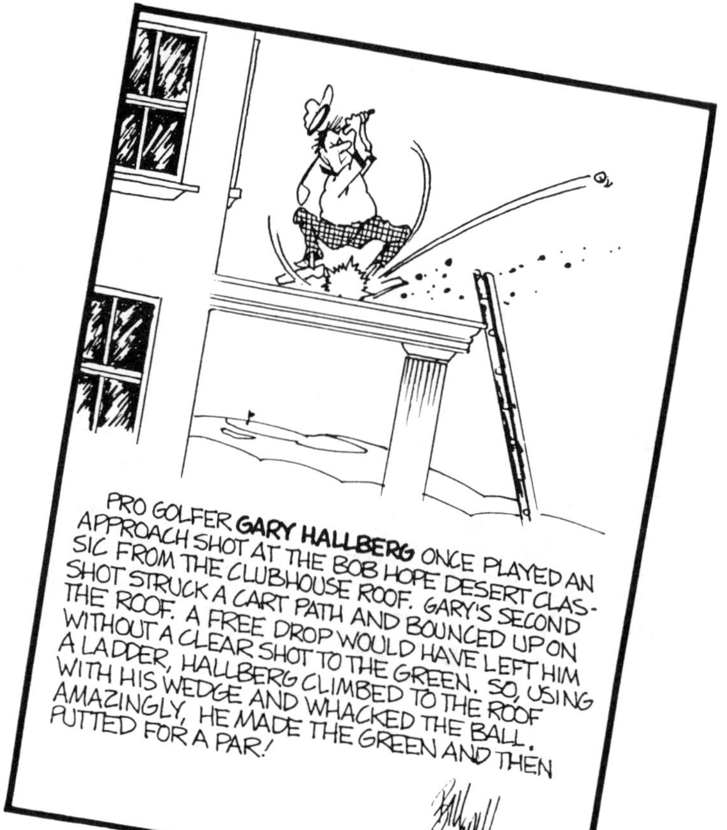

PRO GOLFER **GARY HALLBERG** ONCE PLAYED AN APPROACH SHOT AT THE BOB HOPE DESERT CLAS-SIC FROM THE CLUBHOUSE ROOF. GARY'S SECOND SHOT STRUCK A CART PATH AND BOUNCED UP ON THE ROOF. A FREE DROP WOULD HAVE LEFT HIM WITHOUT A CLEAR SHOT TO THE GREEN. SO, USING A LADDER, HALLBERG CLIMBED TO THE ROOF WITH HIS WEDGE AND WHACKED THE BALL. AMAZINGLY, HE MADE THE GREEN AND THEN PUTTED FOR A PAR!

ENGLISHMAN **BEN SAYERS** NEVER WON THE BRITISH OPEN, BUT HE BECAME A LEGEND AT THE TOURNEY. EVEN THOUGH HE PLAYED IN THE EVENT EVERY YEAR FROM 1880 TO 1923 AND CAME AWAY EMPTY-HANDED, BEN WAS A CROWD PLEASER. THAT'S BECAUSE EVERY TIME HE SANK A BIRDIE PUTT, SAYERS WOULD CELEBRATE BY DOING A CARTWHEEL ON THE GREEN!

A GOLF SHOT THAT RICOCHETED OFF A TREE ENDED UP INSIDE THE BAG ROOM DURING THE 1976 PLEASANT VALLEY CLASSIC IN SUTTON, MASS. BUT FRUSTRATED PRO **LARRY ZIEGLER** DECIDED TO PLAY THE BALL WHERE IT LAY. ZIEGLER'S FIRST SHOT NIPPED A BAG AND BOUNCED AROUND THE ROOM. BUT HIS SECOND CHIP FLEW OUT OF THE ROOM AND LANDED ON THE NINTH GREEN. FOR TRYING TO MAKE A MOCKERY OF THE GAME, LARRY WAS FINED $500.

AT THE 1978 MASTERS, **TOMMY NAKAJIMA** STRUGGLED TO A RECORD-TYING SCORE OF 13 ON—WHAT ELSE?—THE 13TH HOLE. AFTER SENDING HIS DRIVE INTO RAE'S CREEK, HE TOOK A PENALTY DROP AND HIT TO WITHIN 100 YARDS OF THE GREEN. BUT HIS WEDGE SHOT SPLASHED INTO THE CREEK AGAIN. HIS RECOVERY SHOT POPPED UP AND LANDED ON HIS FOOT FOR A TWO-STROKE PENALTY. THEN HE DROPPED HIS CLUB IN THE WATER FOR TWO MORE PENALTY STROKES. AFTER ROCKETING HIS NEXT SHOT OVER THE GREEN, TOMMY FINALLY CHIPPED ON AND TWO-PUTTED FOR HIS EMBARRASSING 13.

YOU COULDN'T BLAME AMATEUR GOLFER BILL GRAVES IF HE ACTED A LITTLE CRABBY AFTER PLAYING A ROUND IN 1985 AT THE DANIA GOLF CLUB IN FLORIDA. A THIEVING LAND CRAB CRAWLED OUT OF ITS HOLE, GRABBED BILL'S BALL ON THE FAIRWAY, AND TOOK IT BACK UNDERGROUND! GRAVES WAS UNABLE TO RECOVER HIS STOLEN BALL, SO HE WAS ALLOWED A FREE DROP WITH ANOTHER BALL.

DURING THE 1935 TEXAS WOMEN'S CLOSED CHAMPIONSHIP, BABE DIDRIKSON ZAHARIAS, WHO NEEDED A PAR ON THE FINAL HOLE, SENT HER APPROACH SHOT INTO THE MUD IN THE ROUGH. BABE MANAGED TO SPLASH THE BALL OUT, BUT SHE LOST HER BALANCE AND FELL INTO THE MUCK. THE MUDDY GOLFER DIDN'T MIND — BECAUSE THE BALL ROLLED ONTO THE GREEN AND INTO THE HOLE FOR AN EAGLE AND THE WIN!

FAMOUS FUNNYMAN **GROUCHO MARX** STRUGGLED WITH THE ACCURSED 16TH HOLE AT FAMED CYPRESS POINT. WHILE PLAYING WITH TV HOST ED SULLIVAN, GROUCHO LAUNCHED FIVE STRAIGHT TEE SHOTS INTO THE BLUE PACIFIC. THEN MARX PICKED UP HIS GOLF BAG, WALKED TO THE EDGE OF THE CLIFF, AND HEAVED HIS BAG INTO THE OCEAN MOANING:

I'VE GOT TO BE THE WORLD'S WORST GOLFER... I HAVE NO RIGHT TO BE ON A COURSE AT ALL!

**JIMMY STEWART** — THE GOLFER, NOT THE ACTOR — WAS FORCED TO PLAY KILLER GOLF DURING THE 1972 SINGAPORE OPEN. STEWART CAME FACE TO FACE WITH A 10-FOOT COBRA ON THE THIRD HOLE, AND BASHED THE SERPENT TO DEATH WITH HIS 3-IRON. BUT THE SUDDEN DEATH MATCH WASN'T OVER. A SMALLER SNAKE SLITHERED FROM THE COBRA'S MOUTH — AND QUICKLY MET A SIMILAR FATE.

AMATEURS **RICHARD BLACKMAN** AND **WILLIAM SMITHLINE** WERE ENJOYING A ROUND OF GOLF DURING THEIR 1986 VACATION IN THE BAHAMAS WHEN THEY STUMBLED UPON AN AFRICAN LION ON THE 16TH TEE. THE FRIGHTENED DUFFERS BLINKED TWICE AND THEN DASHED FOR THE CLUBHOUSE. THE BEAST HAD ESCAPED FROM A NEARBY CIRCUS AND WAS LATER RECAPTURED WITHOUT HARMING ANYONE.

PRO GOLFER JOHNNY MILLER SET AN UNOFFICIAL RECORD BY HITTING THE SAME TREE THREE TIMES ON THE SAME HOLE AT THE 1982 MEMORIAL IN DUBLIN, OHIO. MILLER WAS IN THIRD PLACE JUST ONE STROKE OFF THE LEAD WHEN HE WAS FELLED BY THE TREE ON THE 17TH HOLE. HIS TRIPLE-BOGEY 7 LEFT HIM IN A TIE FOR 22ND.
FOR SHEER ARROGANCE ON THE GOLF COURSE, PRO ARCHIE COMPSTON HAD NO PEER DURING HIS PLAYING DAYS IN THE 1920s AND '30s. COMPSTON EMPLOYED THREE CADDIES — ONE TO TOTE HIS BAG, ANOTHER TO CARRY HIS SWEATER, RAINCOAT, AND UMBRELLA, AND A THIRD WHOSE SOLE RESPONSIBILITY WAS TO TAKE CARE OF HIS PIPE AND TOBACCO.

WILD WITH JOY OVER MAKING A DIFFICULT SHOT DURING THE 1934 U.S. OPEN, CO-LEADER BOBBY CRUIKSHANK THREW HIS CLUB IN THE AIR.
IT LANDED SMACK ON BOBBY'S HEAD,
KNOCKING HIM COLD! NEVER FULLY RECOVERING, BOBBY FINISHED THE TOURNAMENT WITH A THIRD PLACE TIE AND A LUMPY NOGGIN!

U.S. PRO GOLFER KENT KLUBA AND RAPHAEL ALARCON OF MEXICO GOT LOST AT THE 1985 FRENCH OPEN!
PLAYING ALONE WITHOUT A GALLERY, THE PAIR TEED OFF ON THE THIRD HOLE ...OR SO THEY THOUGHT. AS THEY REACHED THE GREEN, THEY DISCOVERED THEY WERE PLAYING THE 13th HOLE! PENALTY: TWO STROKES AND ENDLESS RIBBING!

FLAILING AWAY IN THE BUNKERS LIKE NO COMPETITOR HAD EVER DONE BEFORE, GOLFER **HERMAN TISSIES** RECORDED THE HIGHEST SINGLE-HOLE SCORE IN MODERN BRITISH OPEN HISTORY—A BUNGLING 15! ON THE PAR-3 EIGHTH HOLE AT THE 1950 OPEN, HE BLASTED HIS BALL FROM ONE BUNKER TO ANOTHER FOR *11 STRAIGHT SHOTS* BEFORE GETTING THE BALL ONTO THE GREEN WHERE HE THEN 3-PUTTED.

GOLFER **SUE ELLEN NORTHRUP** USED A WILD DRIVE TO DOWN HER COMPETITOR IN A 1970 MATCH IN FORT LAUDERDALE, FLA. NORTHRUP WAS DRIVING THE GOLF CART TO THE FOURTH TEE WHEN THE ACCELERATOR STUCK. THE VEHICLE SMASHED INTO OPPONENT AUDREY MCDERMOTT, WHO WAS UNABLE TO CONTINUE AND HAD TO FORFEIT THE MATCH.

SHORTLY AFTER WINNING THE U.S. AMATEUR CHAMPIONSHIP IN 1964, GOLFER BARBARA ROMACK WAS INVITED TO PLAY GOLF IN PALM SPRINGS WITH FORMER PRESIDENT DWIGHT EISENHOWER. IKE WAS SITTING IN HIS GOLF CART IN THE ROUGH AHEAD OF ROMACK WAITING FOR HER APPROACH SHOT. TO HER DISMAY, ROMACK SHANKED THE BALL — AND IT FLEW RIGHT THROUGH THE FRONT OF IKE'S CART, BARELY MISSING HIS HEAD. SAID A SHAKEN ROMACK, "I CAME AWFULLY CLOSE TO BEING A PRESIDENTIAL ASSASSIN!"

LEE TREVINO MADE HIS BIGGEST BLUNDER AT THE 1970 BRITISH OPEN. ON THE 5th HOLE, AN UNUSUAL DOUBLE GREEN THAT HAD TWO CUPS FOR TWO SEPARATE HOLES, LEE SENT HIS BALL STRAIGHT FOR THE FLAG — THE WRONG FLAG! AN EMBARRASSED TREVINO THEN THREE-PUTTED FROM 80 FEET FOR A BOGEY.

AS THE THUNDERCLOUDS WERE BUILDING UP BEFORE THE FINAL ROUND OF THE 1940 U.S. OPEN, TWO THREESOMES HURRIED OFF THE FIRST TEE. AFTER THEIR ROUNDS, ALL SIX GOLFERS WERE DISQUALIFIED FOR STARTING 28 MINUTES AHEAD OF THEIR OFFICIAL TEE TIMES ... INCLUDING **PORKY OLIVER**, WHOSE SCORE WOULD HAVE PUT HIM IN A PLAYOFF FOR THE CHAMPIONSHIP!

PLAYING A TOUGH SHOT ATOP LAVA ROCKS AT HAWAII'S MAKENA GOLF COURSE IN 1986, AMATEUR **ELVIN WILSON** STROKED A BALL WHICH RICOCHETED OFF A ROCK AND THEN SEEMED TO DISAPPEAR. WHILE HIS PLAYING PARTNERS SCRATCHED THEIR HEADS IN AMAZEMENT, WILSON ANNOUNCED HE HAD FOUND THE BALL— AND PULLED IT OUT FROM UNDER HIS ARMPIT!

IN ONE OF THE WACKIEST GOLF MATCHES EVER, PROS **WALTER HAGEN** AND **JOE KIRKWOOD** TURNED THE STREETS OF TIJUANA, MEXICO INTO THEIR OWN PERSONAL GOLF COURSE IN 1928. PLAYING FROM THE LOCAL LINKS BACK TO THEIR HOTEL, THE ZANY GOLFERS DODGED TRUCKS, BUSES, AND DONKEY CARTS THROUGH THE STREETS, INTO THE HOTEL LOBBY, AND THEN UP THE STAIRS AND INTO THEIR ROOM. KIRKWOOD WAS THE FIRST TO PITCH HIS BALL INTO THE TOILET BOWL TO WIN THE CRAZY MATCH.

AFTER HIS WIFE THREATENED TO LEAVE HIM IF HE DIDN'T CURB HIS FIERY TEMPER, PRO GOLFER **KY LAFFOON** TOED THE LINE... UNTIL HIS NEXT TOURNAMENT. THEN THE DEPRESSION-ERA GOLFER HIT AN ERRANT SHOT INTO A BED OF HONEYSUCKLE. THREE FUTILE SWINGS LATER, KY UNLEASHED A TORRENT OF SWEAR WORDS THAT SENT HIS EMBARRASSED WIFE SCURRYING FOR THE CLUBHOUSE. HURRYING AFTER HER, A PLEADING LAFFOON EXPLAINED, "I WASN'T CUSSING ABOUT GOLF, DARLING. I JUST HATE HONEYSUCKLE!"

PLAY WAS SO SLOW AT THE 1889 BRITISH OPEN IN MUSSELBURGH, SCOTLAND, THAT SOME GOLFERS WERE FORCED TO FINISH THEIR ROUND BY THE LIGHT OF STREET LAMPS. SCORECARDS WERE CHECKED BY CANDLELIGHT. THOSE PLAYERS WHO HAD NO CHANCE OF WINNING WERE PAID SMALL SUMS OF MONEY TO WITHDRAW IN ORDER TO LET THE FRONTRUNNERS FINISH AT AN EARLIER HOUR.

GOLFING GREAT **BOBBY JONES** ONCE QUIT IN THE MIDDLE OF THE BRITISH OPEN. IN 1921, 19-YEAR-OLD BOBBY BECAME RATTLED BY GALE-FORCE WINDS ON THE THIRD DAY OF PLAY. JONES FINALLY EXPLODED ON THE 11TH HOLE. HE TORE UP HIS SCORECARD, TOSSED THE PIECES INTO THE EDEN RIVER AND STORMED OFF THE NORTHERN ENGLISH COURSE.

THE MOST EAR-SPLITTING GOLF EVENT IN THE WORLD WAS **THE FIRECRACKER TOURNAMENT** — A WACKY FUND-RAISING AFFAIR THAT RAN ANNUALLY FROM THE 1940s INTO THE 1970s IN SPOKANE, WASHINGTON. SCORES SOARED AS HIGH AS ROMAN CANDLES WHEN SPECTATORS, CADDIES, AND PLAYERS SET OFF FIRECRACKERS, SIRENS, BELLS, AND HORNS IN THE MIDDLE OF GOLFERS' SWINGS!

PRO GOLFER **DON JANUARY** SET THE UNOFFICIAL RECORD FOR LOITERING ON A GREEN WHEN HE WAITED A FULL *SEVEN MINUTES*, HOPING HIS TEETERING BALL WOULD DROP INTO THE CUP ON THE 18TH HOLE OF THE 1963 PHOENIX OPEN. THE BALL NEVER FELL. "THE JANUARY RULE" NOW STATES A PLAYER HAS TEN SECONDS TO TAP IN HIS BALL OR FACE A PENALTY STROKE.

11
10
AT THE 1985
U.S. WOMEN'S
OPEN, PRO GOLFER
**JAN STEPHENSON**'S
CHARGE FOR THE LEAD LITERALLY STOPPED
ON A DIME. ON THE 11TH GREEN, JAN MARKED
HER BALL WITH A DIME AND TAPPED IT DOWN
WITH HER PUTTER... BUT THE DIME STUCK TO
THE BOTTOM OF THE CLUB HEAD! AS SHE LIFT-
ED HER CLUB, THE COIN FELL TO THE GREEN.
JAN WAS ASSESSED A PENALTY STROKE,
LOST HER CONCENTRATION AND FALTERED
THROUGHOUT THE REST OF THE TOURNEY.

IN 1974, **NIGEL DENHAM** WAS PLAYING IN THE ENG-
LISH AMATEUR STROKE PLAY COMPETITION WHEN
HE HIT HIS BALL PAST THE 18TH GREEN AND INTO
THE CLUBHOUSE. BECAUSE THE LOCAL RULE
SAID THE CLUBHOUSE WAS IN BOUNDS, DENHAM
PLAYED THE BALL OFF THE CARPET AND CHIPPED
IT OUT THROUGH AN OPEN WINDOW. HE SCORED
A BOGEY 5 ON THE HOLE.

TRAILING BY ONLY ONE SHOT IN THE FINAL ROUND OF THE 1954 MASTERS, PRO GOLFER **JACK BURKE, JR.** HIT HIS SECOND SHOT ON THE PAR 5 15TH HOLE STRAIGHT FOR THE GREEN. BUT A SPECTATOR IN FRONT OF THE GREEN, SCRAMBLING TO GET OUT OF THE WAY OF THE BALL, FELL DOWN. JACK'S BALL HIT THE FAN RIGHT ON THE HEEL OF HIS SHOE AND BOUNCED CLEAR BACK INTO A CREEK! BURKE TOOK A SIX THAT ENDED HIS QUEST FOR THE GREEN JACKET.

NOT ONCE BUT TWICE, PRO GOLFER **COLLEEN WALKER** SIGNED INCORRECT SCORECARDS IN 1986!

IN TORONTO, THE MISTAKE COST COLLEEN A $2,500 PAYCHECK. BUT IN NEW YORK'S MASTERCARD INTERNATIONAL, HER GAFFE COST HER $18,500—AND A 2ND PLACE FINISH!

AMATEUR GOLFER **JOHN REMINGTON** HIT ONE OF THE MOST SHAMEFUL ACES IN ALL OF GOLF. IN 1959, ON THE PAR-3 7TH HOLE AT THE COTSWOLD GOLF CLUB IN ENGLAND, REMINGTON SMACKED A FIVE-IRON THAT RICOCHETED OFF A DRAINAGE PIPE IN THE ROUGH, SKITTERED ACROSS THE GRASS TOWARD A GREENSIDE BUNKER, BOUNCED OFF A RAKE, AND ROLLED ONTO THE GREEN. INCREDIBLY, THE BALL THEN GLANCED OFF THE BALL OF REMINGTON'S PARTNER— AND PLOPPED RIGHT INTO THE HOLE FOR AN OUTRAGEOUS ACE!

IN THE 1965 BING CROSBY PRO-AM, ACTOR **JACK LEMMON** WAS PLAYING TERRIBLY, AVERAGING EIGHT OR NINE STROKES A HOLE. ON THE 18TH GREEN, LEMMON FACED A 35-FOOT PUTT FOR HIS 12TH SHOT ON THE HOLE. TURNING TO HIS CADDIE—A SEASONED VETERAN— FOR ADVICE, JACK ASKED:

STUDENTS AT CASEVILLE (MICH.) HIGH SCHOOL HAD LITTLE TO CHEER ABOUT DURING THE 1990-91 SPORTS SCHEDULE. THE EAGLES' FOOTBALL, BASEBALL, BOYS AND GIRLS BASKETBALL, SOFTBALL, VOLLEYBALL, AND BOYS AND GIRLS TRACK TEAMS ALL WENT WINLESS! ONLY A 4-7 GOLF TEAM PREVENTED A COMPLETE SHUT-OUT FOR THE HAPLESS SCHOOL.
OUR HERO!
HOT-HEADED GOLFER IVAN GANTZ HAD A HISTORY OF BELLY-FLOPPING INTO BUNKERS OR OTHERWISE ABUSING HIMSELF WHEN THINGS WENT WRONG. ONCE AFTER MISSING A SHORT PUTT, HE THREW HIS PUTTER DOWN AND BEGAN SLUGGING HIMSELF IN THE HEAD! GANTZ LATER SAID HE DROPPED THE CLUB FIRST BECAUSE HE DIDN'T WANT TO KILL HIMSELF.

ALL EVEN AFTER 18 HOLES IN THE FINAL ROUND OF THE 1980 CLUB CHAMPIONSHIP AT BOONE GOLF CLUB IN NORTH CAROLINA, **MARGARET McNEIL** AND EARLENA ADAMS HEADED TO THE NEXT TEE FOR THE FIRST HOLE OF SUDDEN DEATH. AS McNEIL TOOK A PRACTICE SWING, HER CLUB ACCIDENTALLY STRUCK ADAMS IN THE LEFT FOREARM AND BROKE IT! SINCE ADAMS COULDN'T CONTINUE, McNEIL WON BY DEFAULT.

**BILLY CASPER** WAS CRUISING ALONG AT THE 1959 CHICAGO OPEN WHEN HIS TEE SHOT ON THE 11TH HOLE LANDED IN THE MIDDLE OF A THICK MULBERRY BUSH. CASPER BEGAN TO HACK AWAY TRYING TO DISLODGE THE BALL— UNAWARE THAT HE COULD HAVE TAKEN A FREE DROP. TEN STROKES LATER, HE FINALLY HOLED OUT. THE FRUSTRATED CASPER LOST THE TOURNEY BY THREE STROKES.

AT THE 1952 PALM BEACH ROUND ROBIN IN NEW ROCHELLE, N.Y., PRO GOLFER **CARY MIDDLECOFF** HIT A DRIVE ON THE 16TH HOLE THAT BOUNCED OFF THE GREEN AND PLOPPED INTO THE JACKET POCKET OF A SPECTATOR WHO PANICKED AND TOOK OFF RUNNING. OFFICIALS MADE MIDDLECOFF PLAY THE BALL FROM WHERE THE FAN FINALLY DROPPED IT 20 YARDS AWAY. MIDDLECOFF DOUBLE-BOGEYED THE HOLE AND FINISHED SECOND IN THE TOURNEY.
16

PRO GOLFER **TED KROLL** DISCOVERED DURING THE 1955 FORT WAYNE OPEN THAT TANGLING WITH BARBED WIRE CAN BE A PAIN IN THE BUTT. ONE OF KROLL'S DRIVES LANDED PERILOUSLY CLOSE TO A BARBED WIRE FENCE. AFTER MAKING A SLIGHT MISCALCULATION, KROLL WENT INTO HIS BACKSWING—AND LET OUT A YELP AS HIS POSTERIOR WAS PIERCED BY THE RAZOR-SHARP BARBS.

CENSORED

DOUBLE CENSORED

CENSORED

SOMETIMES A TYPOGRAPHICAL ERROR CAN BE MORE ACCURATE THAN THE CORRECT WORD. A **NORTH CAROLINA TOURISM BOOKLET** BOASTED OF SUCH FABULOUS GOLF RESORTS AS PINEHURST AND SOUTHERN PINES, "*WHERE IT IS SAID THAT THERE ARE MORE GOLF* CURSES *PER SQUARE MILE THAN ANYWHERE ELSE IN THE WORLD.*" THEN AGAIN, MAYBE THIS WASN'T A TYPO AFTER ALL.

PRO GOLFER **JANE GEDDES** WAS LUCKY TO POCKET A WIN AT THE 1986 BOSTON FIVE CLASSIC AFTER HER WILD TEE SHOT DURING THE FINAL ROUND HEADED STRAIGHT TOWARD A WATER HAZARD. BUT GEDDES BREATHED A SIGH OF RELIEF WHEN THE BALL ENDED UP IN THE SHIRT POCKET OF A STUNNED MALE SPECTATOR. A PACK OF CIGARETTES CUSHIONED THE BLOW AND SAVED GEDDES' SHOT FROM A WATERY FATE.
PLUNK!
ENGLISHMAN **HARRY DEARTH** PLAYED AN ENTIRE ROUND OF GOLF CLAD IN A COMPLETE SUIT OF ARMOR! IN 1912, DEARTH ACCEPTED A CHALLENGE MATCH DRESSED IN FULL KNIGHT REGALIA AND PLAYED AT BUSHEY HALL IN ENGLAND WHERE HE CLANKED TO A 2 AND 1 DEFEAT.

ONCE, AFTER PUTTING BADLY IN THE 1963 WALKER CUP COMPETITION, GOLFER **BILLY JOE PATTON** DECIDED TO TAKE CARE OF THE PROBLEM RIGHT THEN AND THERE. HE DASHED TO THE FIRTH OF FORTH, THE BAY NEXT TO THE OLD COURSE AT FAMED ST. ANDREWS. THERE, PATTON HURLED HIS PUTTER FAR OUT INTO THE WATER AND YELLED:
YOU'LL NEVER THREE PUTT FOR ME AGAIN!
IRONS
WOODS
WHEEEEE!!
DURING A 1951 MATCH IN ARIZONA, AMATEUR GOLFER **DR. H.J. MORLAND** LINED UP HIS PUTT FOR A BIRDIE FOUR, TAPPED THE BALL, THEN WATCHED IN AMAZEMENT AS IT SUDDENLY STOPPED INCHES SHORT OF THE HOLE. THE DOC THEN DISCOVERED THAT AN EARTHWORM HAD SOMEHOW MANAGED TO WRAP ITSELF AROUND THE BALL AND STOPPED IT FROM GOING IN THE HOLE!

GOLFER **ANDREW KIRKALDY** SUFFERED THE WORST DISASTER EVER AT THE BRITISH OPEN. IN 1889, ON THE 14TH HOLE, HE WHIFFED A PUTT ONLY *ONE INCH* AWAY FROM THE CUP! AFTER HIS ONE-HANDED SWIPE FAILED TO TOUCH THE BALL, KIRKALDY MOANED:

IF THE HOLE WERE BIG ENOUGH, I'D BURY MYSELF IN IT!

WHIFF

HE LOST THE OPEN BY ONE STROKE.

FORMER U.S. OPEN CHAMPION **CYRIL WALKER** WAS ONCE ARRESTED FOR SLOW PLAY! DURING THE 1930 LOS ANGELES OPEN, HIS MADDENING DILLY-DALLYING CREATED AN ENORMOUS TRAFFIC JAM FOR THOSE PLAYING BEHIND HIM. WHEN HE IGNORED TOURNAMENT OFFICIALS' PLEAS TO SPEED UP, WALKER WAS DISQUALIFIED. BUT HE REFUSED TO LEAVE THE COURSE. OFFICIALS FINALLY SUMMONED POLICE, WHO GRABBED WALKER BY THE ELBOWS AND CARTED HIM OFF AS HE KICKED AND SCREAMED IN PROTEST.

IN 1983, **HALE IRWIN** MADE THE MOST PITIFUL PUTT IN PRO GOLF... AND IT COST HIM THE BRITISH OPEN. WITH HIS BALL JUST THREE INCHES AWAY FROM THE CUP, HALE TRIED TO TAP IT IN WITH A CASUAL BACKHAND STROKE ...AND WHIFFED THE BALL! HE LOST THE TOURNAMENT BY ONE STROKE.

BASEBALL GREAT **MICKEY MANTLE** PUT ON A DISPLAY OF CLUB ABUSE DURING A BING CROSBY PRO-AMATEUR EVENT IN THE 1950s. AFTER TOPPING HIS BALL ON AN EARLY HOLE, MANTLE SNAPPED HIS 3-IRON IN RAGE. THEN ON THE 11TH HOLE, MICKEY BLASTED HIS BALL OUT OF BOUNDS—AND THEN BENT ANOTHER 3-IRON AROUND A TREE. MANTLE INFORMED HIS PLAYING PARTNER THAT HE CARRIED SIX 3-IRONS WITH HIM—BECAUSE HE HATES THEM!

COMEDIAN **JACKIE GLEASON** LOVED GOLF SO MUCH HE HAD HIS SPECIAL CART CUSTOMIZED TO INCLUDE A TELEPHONE, TELEVISION, REFRIGERATOR, AND TWO-WAY RADIO. DURING ONE MATCH, GLEASON'S CART SLIPPED INTO GEAR AND ROLLED DOWN A BANK INTO A POND. THE UNFLAPPABLE "GREAT ONE" GLANCED OVER AT THE SUBMERGED CART AND NOTED, *"WELL, THERE GO MY CIGARETTES."*

PRO GOLFER **KEN GREEN** PACKED HIS VAN AND DROVE HIS CADDIE, MOTHER, SISTER, SON, NIECE, AND TWO DOGS TO THE 1986 CANADIAN OPEN. GREEN CHECKED EVERYONE INTO THEIR HOTEL ROOMS FOLLOWING THE 8½ HOUR DRIVE—AND THEN SUDDENLY REALIZED HE HAD FORGOTTEN ONE THING. HE HAD FORGOTTEN TO ENTER THE TOURNAMENT! KEN HAD NO CHOICE BUT TO PACK EVERYONE UP, TURN AROUND AND HEAD BACK HOME.

**REX CALDWELL**'S CADDIE SHOULD HAVE RECEIVED COMBAT PAY—OR AT LEAST A PURPLE HEART—FOLLOWING THE 1987 AT&T PEBBLE BEACH NATIONAL PRO-AM. BACK-TO-BACK EMBARRASSING ACCIDENTS OCCURRED WHEN CALDWELL FIRST NAILED CADDIE "LOST LEE" STEHLE IN THE CHEST WITH A RICOCHET SHOT OFF THE BRANCH OF A TREE, AND THEN ACCIDENTALLY SMACKED HIM IN THE FACE WITH HIS WEDGE WHILE SLAMMING THE CLUB DOWN INTO HIS GOLF BAG!

IN THE 1965 BING CROSBY PRO-AM, AMATEUR **MATT PALACIO** HIT A DRIVE ON THE SEASIDE 18TH IN THE GENERAL DIRECTION OF JAPAN. "*ONLY GOD CAN SAVE THAT ONE,*" PALACIO MUTTERED. JUST THEN, THE WAVES RECEDED. THE BALL STRUCK A BARE ROCK AND MIRACULOUSLY CAROMED BACK ONTO THE FAIRWAY. GAZING AT THE HEAVENS, PALACIO SHOUTED:

THANK YOU, GOD!

MILWAUKEE POSTAL WORKER **WALTER DANECKI** WAS VACATIONING IN ENGLAND WHEN HE BLUFFED HIS WAY INTO THE 1965 BRITISH OPEN. DANECKI QUICKLY SHOWED THAT HIS BEST ROUNDS WERE BACK HOME ON HIS MAIL ROUTE. A HIGH HANDI-CAP PLAYER, HE WENT OUT AND SHOT QUALIFYING ROUNDS OF 108 AND 113 FOR A TOTAL OF 81 OVER PAR!

SHORTLY AFTER WINNING THE BEST SUPPORTING ACTOR AWARD FOR HIS ROLE OF THE KINDLY PRIEST IN "GOING MY WAY" IN 1944, **BARRY FITZGERALD** ACCIDENTALLY DECAPITATED HIS OSCAR WHILE HE WAS PRACTICING HIS GOLF SWING IN HIS HOUSE. BECAUSE IT WAS WARTIME, THE COVETED STATUETTE WAS MADE OF PLASTER AND BROKE EASILY. PARAMOUNT PAID $10 TO REPLACE IT.

FAITH AND BEGORRAH!

**TOMMY BOLT** WAS LEGENDARY FOR HIS FITS OF RAGE ON THE GOLF COURSE. ONCE, AFTER A BAD DRIVE, HE STOMPED SO HARD ON THE HEAD OF HIS DRIVER THAT IT CAUGHT IN HIS SPIKES AND HE COULDN'T REMOVE IT. AS PLAYERS AND FANS MOVED DOWN THE FAIRWAY, TOMMY COULD ONLY STAND THERE AND YELL FOR HELP. FINALLY, A FELLOW COMPETITOR RACED BACK AND YANKED THE DRIVER OFF BOLT'S SHOE.

WHILE PLAYING GOLF WITH BOB HOPE, MOVIE PRODUCER **SAM GOLDWYN** BLEW AN EASY PUTT. IN A RAGE, HE HURLED HIS PUTTER INTO A BUSH, VOWING NEVER TO USE THAT CLUB AGAIN. HOPE THEN QUIETLY PICKED UP THE DISCARDED PUTTER AND USED IT ON THE NEXT HOLE TO SINK A 20-FOOTER. IMPRESSED, GOLDWYN TRIED A FEW PRACTICE PUTTS WITH THE CLUB AND THEN ASKED TO BUY IT FROM HOPE. WHEN THE COMEDIAN AGREED, GOLDWYN HAPPILY, BUT UNWITTINGLY, BOUGHT BACK HIS OWN PUTTER FOR $50!

GOLFER **JOHNNY DE FOREST** PUT HIS WRONG FOOT FORWARD AFTER WHACKING HIS BALL INTO THE BANK OF A CREEK DURING THE THIRD ROUND OF THE 1953 MASTERS. DE FOREST CAREFULLY REMOVED HIS LEFT SHOE AND SOCK, PLANTED HIS BARE FOOT ON THE BANK—AND IN HIS FLIGHTINESS, STEPPED INTO THE WATER WITH HIS RIGHT SHOE!

IN 1913, DURING A QUALIFYING ROUND OF THE SHAWNEE INVITATIONAL GOLF TOURNAMENT FOR LADIES, MRS J. F. MEEHAN OF PHILADELPHIA SET A STAND-TILL-DOOMSDAY RECORD FOR TOURNAMENT GOLF. HITTING HER DRIVE ON THE PAR-3 16TH HOLE INTO THE BINNIEKILL RIVER, MRS. MEEHAN AND HER HUSBAND COMMANDEERED A ROWBOAT TO PURSUE THE FLOATING BALL. SLAPPING AND FLAILING, SHE FINALLY BEACHED THE ELUSIVE BALL ...40 STROKES LATER. FROM THERE (AND THROUGH THE WOODS) SHE TOOK A MERE 120 STROKES — HOLING HER PUTT ON STROKE 161 IN GOLF'S MOST RIDICULOUS PERFORMANCE!

ONE OF THE ROUGHEST GOLF COURSES IN THE WORLD IS **YELLOWKNIFE**, IN CANADA'S FRIGID NORTHWEST TERRITORIES. GOLFERS ARE FACED WITH A COURSE MADE ENTIRELY OF SAND WITH TINY PATCHES OF GRASS SPROUTING HERE AND THERE. THEN THERE ARE THE SWARMS OF MOSQUITOES AND BLACK FLIES—AND THE THIEVING RAVENS WHO SWOOP DOWN AND STEAL BALLS DESPITE THE SHOUTS OF ANGRY GOLFERS. NESTS CRAMMED WITH MORE THAN 100 BALLS HAVE BEEN FOUND NEAR THE COURSE!

GANGSTER **AL CAPONE** SELDOM SHOT PAR WHILE PLAYING GOLF—BUT IN 1928 HE MANAGED TO SHOOT HIMSELF. SCARFACE CARRIED A LOADED REVOLVER IN HIS GOLF BAG WHILE PLAYING AT THE BURNHAM WOODS GOLF COURSE NEAR CHICAGO. ONE OF HIS CLUBS JARRED THE TRIGGER OF THE GUN AND IT DISCHARGED, SHOOTING CAPONE IN THE FOOT! THE HOWLING GANGSTER HOPPED AROUND ON ONE FOOT UNTIL HIS BODYGUARDS RUSHED HIM TO THE HOSPITAL.

IN THE 1986 U.S. OPEN, **BEN CRENSHAW**'S BALL LODGED IN A BUSH, SO HE DECLARED IT UNPLAYABLE AND DROPPED IT. SEEING THAT THE BALL WAS GOING TO ROLL MORE THAN TWO CLUB-LENGTHS—WHICH REQUIRES A RE-DROP—BEN PICKED UP THE BALL WHILE IT WAS STILL MOVING. *"I WISH I HADN'T SEEN THAT,"* SAID AN OFFICIAL, WHO PENALIZED CRENSHAW TWO COSTLY STROKES—DROPPING HIM FROM A FIFTH-PLACE FINISH TO SIXTH.

**ED DUDLEY** WAS BATTLING FOR THE LEAD IN THE 1937 MASTERS WHEN HE LAUNCHED A PICTURE-PERFECT DRIVE DOWN THE 13TH FAIRWAY. UNFORTUNATELY, A SPECTATOR PICKED THAT EXACT TIME TO RACE ACROSS THE COURSE. HE WAS STRUCK SQUARE ON THE HEAD WITH THE BALL WHICH THEN CAROMED INTO A NEARBY CREEK. DUDLEY DOUBLE-BOGEYED THE HOLE AND FINISHED THIRD.

IN THE 1978 DRYDEN INVITATIONAL GOLF TOURNAMEN IN TEXAS, **T.J. MOORE** BLASTED 20 STRAIGHT SHOTS INTO A POND AT THE 18TH HOLE — AND RACKED UP A MORTIFYING 46 STROKES ON THE PAR-4 HOLE! T.J. HAD TO BORROW BALLS FROM OTHER GOLFERS TO FINISH THE HOLE.

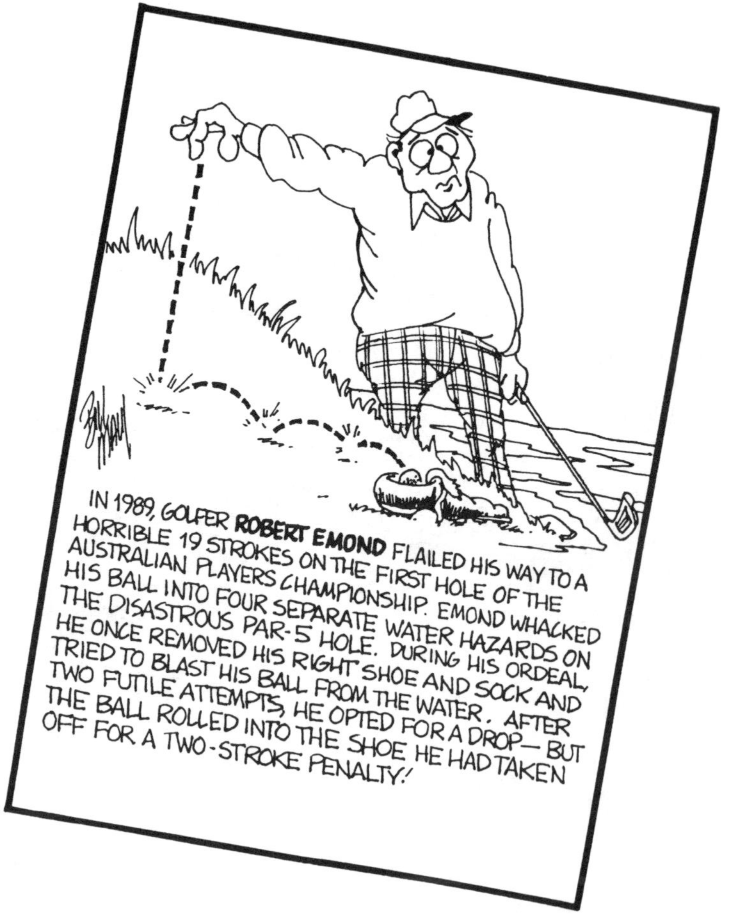

IN 1989, GOLFER **ROBERT EMOND** FLAILED HIS WAY TO A HORRIBLE 19 STROKES ON THE FIRST HOLE OF THE AUSTRALIAN PLAYERS CHAMPIONSHIP. EMOND WHACKED HIS BALL INTO FOUR SEPARATE WATER HAZARDS ON THE DISASTROUS PAR-5 HOLE. DURING HIS ORDEAL, HE ONCE REMOVED HIS RIGHT SHOE AND SOCK AND TRIED TO BLAST HIS BALL FROM THE WATER. AFTER TWO FUTILE ATTEMPTS, HE OPTED FOR A DROP— BUT THE BALL ROLLED INTO THE SHOE HE HAD TAKEN OFF FOR A TWO-STROKE PENALTY!

AT THE 1959 BUICK OPEN, SAM SNEAD TAPPED IN A ONE-INCH PUTT WITH ONE HAND — WHILE HOLDING THE FLAGSTICK WITH THE OTHER. THE MANUEVER EARNED SNEAD A TWO-STROKE PENALTY FOR "HITTING AN ATTENDED FLAG-STICK." THE BOO-BOO COST THE UNTHINKING VETERAN A FOURTH-PLACE FINISH IN THE TOURNEY.
PRO GOLFER KEN GREEN IS CALLED "FLY" BECAUSE HE THROWS HIS CLUBS AS IF THEY WERE CHICKEN BONES HEADED TO THE TRASH CAN. DURING THE 1989 PLAYERS CHAMPIONSHIP, GREEN WAS FINED $500 BY A PGA OFFICIAL WHO WATCHED HIM ANGRILY TOSS HIS CLUB INTO A WATER HAZARD. AN UNAPOLOGETIC GREEN NOTED:
THAT PUTTER HAD TO DIE, NEEDED TO DIE. I EITHER GIVE 'EM AWAY OR THEY DIE AN UGLY DEATH!
GLUG! GLUG!

THE MOST FAMOUS HUSTLER TO COME OUT OF THE TENISON PARK MUNICIPAL GOLF COURSE IN EAST DALLAS WAS **LEE TREVINO**. DURING THE 1960s, THE FORMER CADDIE USED A TAPED-UP DR PEPPER SODA BOTTLE TO BEAT OTHER GOLFERS USING REGULAR CLUBS! TREVINO WOULD TEE OFF BY TOSSING THE BALL IN THE AIR AND WHACKING IT LIKE A BASEBALL WITH HIS BOTTLE. FOR PUTTS, HE'D USE THE BOTTLE LIKE A POOL STICK TO SHOOT THE BALL INTO THE HOLE.

PRO GOLFER **SANDRA HAYNIE** MADE QUITE A SPLASH DURING A SUDDEN-DEATH PLAYOFF WITH JOANNE CARNER AT THE 1982 HENREDON CLASSIC. PLAYING HER APPROACH SHOT ON THE EDGE OF A CREEK, HAYNIE LOST HER BALANCE AND PLUNGED FIVE FEET INTO THE WATER HAZARD. A WET HAYNIE COMPLETED THE HOLE BUT LOST THE MATCH.

**FOUR ABERDEEN UNIVERSITY STUDENTS** TRIED TO GOLF THEIR WAY UP SCOTLAND'S 4,406-FOOT MT. BEN NEVIS IN 1961. BUT THEY HAD TO CONCEDE VICTORY TO THE MOUNTAIN. THEY QUIT AFTER LOSING 663 BALLS AND TAKING 1,659 STROKES.

IN 1929, BROTHERS **CLYDE** AND **HAROLD McWHIRTER** PLAYED A LONG-DISTANCE GOLF MATCH BETWEEN SPARTANBURG AND UNION, SOUTH CAROLINA. THE BROTHERS COVERED THE 37-MILE DISTANCE IN 13 HOURS. CLYDE TOOK 780 SHOTS, WHILE HAROLD NEEDED 825. THE McWHIRTERS LOST 22 BALLS BETWEEN THEM AND USED EIGHT CADDIES.

DURING A QUALIFYING ROUND OF THE 1977 U.S. OPEN, **WAYNE LEVI** SOCKED A TEE SHOT OUT OF BOUNDS. HE WAS SO ANGRY WITH HIMSELF THAT HE GRABBED HIS DRIVER AROUND THE NECK AND BEGAN TO STRANGLE IT, SHAKING IT IN FRONT OF HIS FACE. THE SHAFT FLEXED AND THE HEAD OF THE DRIVER SMACKED LEVI RIGHT IN THE MOUTH, LOOSENING A TOOTH AND SLICING HIS LIP. TO MAKE MATTERS WORSE, LEVI MISSED THE CUT.

GOLFER **JOHN ADAMS** HOPPED A TRAIN FOR THE 1922 BRITISH OPEN, BUT WAS SHOCKED TO LEARN THE LOCOMOTIVE DIDN'T STOP AT THE PRESTWICK COURSE. THE TRACKS RAN ALONGSIDE THE FIRST HOLE, SO THE PANICKY COMPETITOR YELLED TO TOURNEY OFFICIALS FROM THE SPEEDING TRAIN THAT HE'D RETURN AS SOON AS HE COULD. BUT ADAMS NEVER MADE HIS STARTING TIME AND WAS DISQUALIFIED — DUE TO POOR "TRAINING."

DURING THE 1939 THOMASVILLE OPEN IN GEORGIA, A **BUMBLING CADDIE** COST GOLFER ROD MUNDAY A SENSATIONAL SHOT FROM OUT OF A SAND TRAP. MUNDAY HAD STROKED HIS BALL PERFECTLY FROM A DEEP BUNKER ON THE 18TH HOLE. THE CADDIE PULLED THE FLAG AND IN THE PROCESS WHACKED THE BOUNCING BALL 40 YARDS AWAY FROM THE HOLE! MUNDAY WOUND UP WITH A QUADRUPLE BOGEY 8.

IN 1986, AMATEUR **BOB GILLMORE**'S TEE SHOT ON THE FIRST HOLE AT THE TERRY HILLS COUNTRY CLUB IN BATAVIA, N.Y., WAS A LOW SCREECHER THAT SMACKED THE WOMEN'S TEE MARKER DIRECTLY IN FRONT OF HIM. THE RICOCHETING BALL FLEW BACK TOWARD GILLMORE — WHO THEN REACHED OUT AND SNAGGED HIS OWN DRIVE ON THE FLY!

**JANICE IRBY** PROVIDED A BIRTHDAY BLAST FOR HER GOLF-FANATIC HUSBAND JOHN BY SLIPPING SEVERAL GOLF BALLS INTO HIS CAKE BEFORE PUTTING IT INTO THE OVEN. JOHN WILL NEVER FORGET THE DAY IN 1987 WHEN HE TURNED 30 — BECAUSE THE HEATED BALLS EXPLODED, SHOOTING CAKE ALL OVER THE OVEN AND SENDING THE SMELL OF BURNING RUBBER THROUGHOUT THE IRBY'S HOME IN CASSELTON, NORTH DAKOTA!

DURING THE 1982 WORLD SERIES OF GOLF, **JERRY PATE** FACED A 50-FOOT PUTT FOR AN EAGLE. HIS FIRST PUTT ROLLED FOUR FEET PAST THE HOLE. SO DID HIS SECOND ONE. HIS THIRD PUTT LIPPED OUT. JERRY THEN TRIED A BACKHAND TAP THAT RIMMED THE CUP AND STRUCK HIM ON THE FOOT FOR A TWO-STROKE PENALTY. THE SELF-DESTRUCTING PATE, WHO HAD BEEN PUTTING FOR A THREE, FINALLY HOLED OUT FOR A QUADRUPLE-BOGEY NINE!

**BERT McMILLAN** WAS LITERALLY KNOCKED OUT OF THE 1950 WEST OF SCOTLAND TOURNAMENT. FINDING HIS BALL LODGED BETWEEN TWO ROCKS, McMILLAN TOOK OUT AN IRON AND GAVE HIS BALL A WHACK. THE BALL DIDN'T MOVE, BUT THE CLUB REBOUNDED OFF THE ROCKS AND STRUCK McMILLAN IN THE HEAD WITH SUCH FORCE THAT HE WAS KNOCKED OUT COLD. ALTHOUGH BERT WASN'T SERIOUSLY INJURED, HE QUIT THE TOURNEY.

HE WASN'T DRINKING, BUT HITTING THE BOTTLE COST IRISH GOLFER **HARRY BRADSHAW** THE 1949 BRITISH OPEN. BRADSHAW'S DRIVE INTO THE ROUGH LANDED IN A BEER BOTTLE THAT WAS STANDING UPRIGHT WITH ITS NECK BROKEN OFF. RATHER THAN TAKE A FREE DROP, HE CHOSE TO PLAY THE BOTTLE AND THE BALL. THE GLASS SHATTERED AND SO DID BRADSHAW'S COMPOSURE WHEN THE BALL MOVED ONLY 25 YARDS. HARRY TOOK A COSTLY DOUBLE-BOGEY 6 ON THE HOLE AND WOUND UP LOSING THE OPEN IN A PLAYOFF.

IN THE MOST NOTORIOUS MENTAL LAPSE EVER IN THE HISTORY OF THE BRITISH OPEN, **ROGER WETHERED** FORGOT WHERE HIS BALL LAY AND ACCIDENTALLY STEPPED ON IT. THE RESULTANT PENALTY STROKE PROVED VERY COSTLY — BECAUSE WITHOUT IT, HE WOULD HAVE WON THE 1921 TOURNAMENT. INSTEAD, WETHERED WOUND UP IN A PLAYOFF WHICH HE LOST.

GOLF HUSTLER **JOHN "MYSTERIOUS" MONTAGUE** USED A RAKE, A SHOVEL, AND A BASEBALL BAT TO DEFEAT BING CROSBY IN A ZANY 1935 MATCH AT THE LAKESIDE COUNTRY CLUB IN NORTH HOLLYWOOD. FOR HIS DRIVE, MONTAGUE THREW THE BALL UP IN THE AIR AND HIT IT WITH HIS BAT. WITH THE SHOVEL, HE SCOOPED THE BALL ONTO THE GREEN FROM THE BUNKER AND THEN USED THE RAKE WITH THE PRONGS POINTED UP AS A PUTTER. HE HAD THE CROONER SINGING THE BLUES — BING QUIT AFTER MONTAGUE BIRDIED THE FIRST HOLE.

**BARB THOMAS** WAS SO FRUSTRATED WITH HER PUTTING AT THE 1986 KONICA SAN JOSE CLASSIC THAT SHE PITCHED HER PUTTER INTO A TRASH CAN—AND LOST IT. THOMAS EXPECTED HER CADDIE TO FISH THE CLUB OUT, BUT HE DIDN'T SEE HER DUMP THE PUTTER. BY THE TIME THE LOSS WAS DISCOVERED AT THE NEXT HOLE, IT WAS TOO LATE. A FAN HAD GRABBED THE PUTTER FOR A SOUVENIR.

A DEVILISH YOUNGSTER LITERALLY STOLE A MATCH FROM GOLFER **CHRISTY O'CONNOR, JR.** IN THE 1972 PENFOLD TOURNAMENT AT QUEEN'S PARK, ENGLAND. NO ONE TOLD O'CONNOR THAT A YOUNG BOY HAD BOLTED ONTO THE COURSE, SNATCHED HIS BALL, AND FLED. SO INSTEAD OF REPLACING THE BALL WITH NO PENALTY, O'CONNOR TOOK A PENALTY STROKE FOR A LOST BALL. HE WOULD HAVE WON OUTRIGHT BUT THAT EXTRA STROKE FORCED HIM INTO A PLAYOFF WHICH HE LOST.

WHILE PLAYING ON THE QUEEN'S COURSE AT GLENEAGLES, SCOTLAND, **MRS. GEORGE SMITH**, THE WIFE OF A USGA OFFICIAL, SENT HER TEE SHOT ON THE 13TH HOLE INTO A THICK STAND OF HEATHER. AFTER SHE AND HER CADDIE SEARCHED FOR SEVERAL MINUTES, MRS. SMITH DECLARED THE BALL LOST— BUT THE CADDIE KEPT LOOKING. WHEN SHE TOLD THE CADDIE...

YOU CAN STOP LOOKING FOR THE BALL NOW.

HE REPLIED...

IT'S NOT THE BALL I'M LOOKING FER, MUM. IT'S YER CLUBS I'VE LOST!

PRO GOLFER **MARK CALCAVECCHIA** WITHDREW FROM THE RAIN-DRENCHED 1986 KEMPER OPEN — BECAUSE HE WAS TOO DIRTY. CALCAVECCHIA WAS INCHING HIS WAY DOWN THE MUDDY BANK OF A STEEP GULLEY FOR A SHOT WHEN HIS FOOTING GAVE WAY. HE SLID SPREAD-EAGLED RIGHT INTO HIS BALL, KNOCKING IT FROM ITS LIE! MARK WAS ASSESSED A 2-STROKE PENALTY FOR MOVING HIS BALL. THE MUD-SPLATTERED GOLFER EVENTUALLY CALLED IT QUITS AFTER THE FRONT NINE AND HEADED TO THE SHOWERS.

IT FLEW IN THE FACE OF GOLFING ETIQUETTE, BUT AN ATLANTA COUNTRY CLUB STAGED A CLUB-TOSSING COMPETITION IN 1936. THE 60 ENTRANTS HEAVED THEIR CLUBS FOR DISTANCE, HEIGHT, STYLE, AND ACCURACY. **RANDOLPH TIMMERMAN** TOOK THE LONG-DISTANCE AWARD FOR HIS AMAZING 61-YARD FLING WHILE **JULIUS HUGHES**'S CLUB SOARED THE HIGHEST WITH HIS HURL OF 100 FEET.

IN ONE OF THE MOST ATROCIOUS PUTTING PERFORMANCES EVER, **BRIAN BARNES** TOOK AN INCREDIBLE 12 STROKES WHILE PUTTING FROM ONLY THREE FEET AWAY FROM THE CUP AT THE 1968 FRENCH OPEN. ON THE EIGHTH GREEN, THE SHORT-TEMPERED BARNES MISSED AN EASY PUTT. THEN HE TRIED TO RAKE THE BALL IN. WHEN THAT FAILED, HE HIT THE BALL BACK AND FORTH WHILE IT WAS STILL MOVING. ADDING PUTTS AND PENALTY STROKES, HE SCORED A DISASTROUS 15 ON THE PAR-3 HOLE!

PLOP!

CRACK!

**AUBREY BOOMER** WAS PLAYING THE EIGHTH HOLE AT ST. ANNE'S GOLF COURSE IN SCOTLAND IN 1923 WHEN HE LOST SIGHT OF THE BALL AFTER HITTING HIS THIRD SHOT STRAIGHT UP IN THE AIR. A SEARCH PROVED UNSUCCESSFUL AND OFFICIALS WERE PREPARED TO HAND BOOMER A PENALTY FOR LOSING HIS BALL. BUT THE STARTLED GOLFER FELT A SOLID OBJECT IN THE RIGHT-HAND POCKET OF HIS JACKET, REACHED IN — AND PRODUCED THE MISSING GOLF BALL!

BRITISH BRONZE MEDALIST **STAN VICKERS** GOT MUCH MORE THAN HE BARGAINED FOR WHEN HE SAT DOWN FOR A REST AFTER COMPETING IN THE 1960 OLYMPIC GAMES' 20-KILOMETER WALK IN ROME. THE EXHAUSTED THIRD-PLACE FINISHER WAS SUDDENLY WHISKED AWAY BY A NON-ENGLISH SPEAKING AMBULANCE CREW WHO THOUGHT HE WAS SICK! THEY SPED THEIR PROTESTING PATIENT TO A NEARBY HOSPITAL WHERE HE REMAINED FOR SEVERAL HOURS BEFORE BRITISH OFFICIALS DISCOVERED WHAT HAD HAPPENED TO THEIR MISSING MEDAL WINNER.

PRO GOLFER **DAVE BALLY** LANDED HIS TEE SHOT ABOUT 15 FEET FROM THE CUP—YET HAD THE MISFORTUNE OF TAKING A TRIPLE BOGEY ON THE PAR-3-HOLE AT THE 1988 CANADIAN OPEN. BALLY WAS STRIDING CONFIDENTLY TOWARD HIS BALL WITH PUTTER IN HAND WHEN HE TRIPPED. DAVE WATCHED HORRIFIED AS HIS CLUB STRUCK THE BALL, SENDING IT CAREENING OFF THE GREEN AND INTO A NEARBY POND!

GOLFERS ARE URGED TO BEAR WITH THE RULES OR RUN THE RISK OF DANGER AT THE **JASPER PARK LODGE GOLF COURSE** IN ALBERTA, CANADA. IT SEEMS THE SOFT, CUSHIONY PUTTING GREENS HAVE BEEN FOUND TO BE COMFORTABLE SPOTS FOR BEARS TO SOAK UP THE SUN'S RAYS AFTER THEIR LONG WINTER NAPS. THE SITUATION BECAME ALMOST UNBEARABLE UNTIL COURSE OFFICIALS RECRUITED A COLLIE NAMED WOLF TO DRIVE THE UNWANTED GUESTS AWAY FROM THE GREENS.

THE GALLERY AT THE 1984 MEMPHIS CLASSIC SAW MORE OF **GARY McCORD** THAN EITHER THEY OR HE WANTED—WHEN THE GOLFER'S PANTS SPLIT WIDE OPEN. McCORD TURNED THE TOURNEY INTO A SKINS GAME BECAUSE HE WASN'T WEARING ANY UNDERWEAR! SCAMPERING FOR ANY KIND OF COVER, GARY WRAPPED HIS CADDIE'S TOWEL AROUND HIS WAIST, BEFORE FINDING ANOTHER COMPETITOR WILLING TO PART WITH HIS RAIN PANTS—FOR A SMALL FEE OF $20.

DURING THE 1961 CANADIAN OPEN, PRO **JIM FERREE** WAS AGGRAVATED BY HIS POOR PUTTING, A NAGGING BACKACHE, AND RAINY WEATHER. SO HE STOPPED IN THE MIDDLE OF A SMALL BRIDGE—AND TOSSED HIS BAG AND CLUBS OVER THE RAIL! BUT WHEN OFFICIALS TOLD HIM HE COULD FACE FINES TOTALING $1,650, FERREE QUICKLY RETRIEVED HIS GEAR AND QUIETLY CONTINUED THE TOURNEY.

TWANG!
TWING!
IN THE 1919 U.S. OPEN PLAYED AT BRAE BURN CC IN WEST NEWTON, MASS., SCOTTISH PRO GOLFER **WILLIE CHISHOLM** SET THE TOURNAMENT RECORD IN FUTILITY FOR A PAR 3 HOLE — 18 STROKES!
AFTER HIS TEE SHOT CAME TO REST AGAINST A BOULDER, THE SCOT DECIDED TO TRY TO HIT IT OUT RATHER THAN TAKE A ONE-STROKE PENALTY FOR AN UNPLAYABLE LIE. AS HE HACKED AWAY AT THE BALL, THE SPARKS FLEW AND THE RINGING OF METAL STRIKING STONE FILLED THE AIR. AFTER NEARLY 30 MINUTES OF FRUSTRATION, WILLIE FINALLY HOLED OUT — BUT THEN COULDN'T REMEMBER HOW MANY STROKES HE HAD TAKEN. WHEN PLAYING PARTNER JIM BARNES INFORMED HIM IT WAS 18, A SHOCKED CHISHOLM SAID, "OH, JIM, THAT CAN'T BE SO. YOU MUST HAVE COUNTED THE ECHOES!"
BILL MCLEAN

THE BIGGEST GOLF TOURNEY—IN NAME AND IN SHAME—HAD TO BE THE **INTERNATIONAL TOURNAMENT FOR DISCRIMINATED AGAINST GOLFERS WHO DON'T LOOK GOOD BUT WOULD LIKE TO BE FELT WANTED ANYHOW OPEN**. FROM 1967 THROUGH 1970, SOME OF THE WORLD'S WORST DUFFERS FLOCKED TO FREDERICK, OKLA., FOR THE "ITFDAGWDLGBWLTBFWA OPEN."

GOLFER **TONEY PENNA** WAS PUTTING FOR A TWO-STROKE LEAD AT THE INTERNATIONAL FOUR-BALL MATCHES IN MIAMI WHEN HE DEVELOPED A TWITCH IN HIS BACKSWING—AND HIT HIS BALL THE WRONG WAY! THE GALLERY AND PENNA'S PLAYING PARTNER HERMAN BARRON STOOD WIDE-EYED AND SILENT OVER WHAT HAD HAPPENED. THE GLITCH ALLOWED THE TEAM OF GENE SARAZEN AND BEN HOGAN THE BREAK THEY NEEDED TO WIN THE TOURNEY.

GOLFING GREAT **BOBBY JONES** HAD TO PAY ADMISSION IN ORDER TO PLAY THE FINAL ROUND OF THE 1926 BRITISH OPEN! JONES WAS IN SECOND PLACE TWO SHOTS BEHIND THE LEADER WHEN HE RETIRED TO HIS HOTEL ROOM FOR A REST. WHEN HE RETURNED TO THE COURSE, HE REALIZED THAT HE'D FORGOTTEN HIS CONTESTANT'S BADGE. THE ENTRANCE GUARD DIDN'T RECOGNIZE HIM AND REFUSED TO LET HIM IN, SO BOBBY JUMPED IN LINE, PAID HIS WAY INTO THE FINAL ROUND, AND WON BY TWO STROKES.

IN THE QUALIFYING COMPETITION FOR THE 1976 BRITISH OPEN, **MAURICE FLITCROFT** TOOK 121 STROKES TO FINISH THE FIRST ROUND—AND THEN QUICKLY WITHDREW. "*I HAD NO CHANCE OF QUALIFYING*," SAID FLITCROFT, A 46-YEAR-OLD CRANE OPERATOR WHO HAD CONNED HIS WAY INTO THE TOURNEY. OPEN OFFICIALS REFUNDED THE ENTRY FEES TO THE TWO MEN WHO WERE FORCED TO PLAY THE MARATHON ROUND WITH HIM.

A LOCAL RULE AT THE **GLEN CANYON GOLF COURSE** IN ARIZONA IS GUARANTEED TO KEEP THE GOLFERS' EYES GLUED TO THE GROUND. DARING DUFFERS ARE ADVISED: *"IF YOUR BALL LANDS WITHIN A CLUB'S LENGTH OF A RATTLESNAKE, YOU ARE ALLOWED TO MOVE THE BALL."*

TALK ABOUT RATTLING THE PLAYERS!

THE FIRST TIME THAT **FRANK SINATRA** PLAYED GOLF WITH ARNOLD PALMER IN PALM SPRINGS, OLD BLUE EYES SPENT MORE TIME IN THE ROUGH THAN IN THE FAIRWAYS. AFTER THE ROUND, WHEN SINATRA ASKED PALMER, "WHAT DO YOU THINK OF MY GAME?" ARNIE REPLIED, "NOT BAD... BUT I STILL PREFER GOLF."

DURING THE 1946 WESTERN AMATEUR, GOLFERS **FRANK STRANAHAN** AND **SMILEY QUICK** TOOK PART IN ONE OF THE MOST MEAN-SPIRITED CHAMPIONSHIP MATCHES EVER. BOMBARDING EACH OTHER WITH INSULTS AND THREATS OF PHYSICAL VIOLENCE, THE GOLFERS STOOD IN THE LINES OF EACH OTHER'S PUTTS, MOVED ABOUT JUST AS THE OTHER WAS PUTTING, AND JINGLED CHANGE IN THEIR POCKETS ON THE OPPONENT'S BACKSWING! STRANAHAN'S 12-FOOT PUTT IN SUDDEN DEATH PUT AN END TO THEIR SORRY PERFORMANCE.

GOLFING SPECTATOR **DAVID HALLE** WAS ONLY LOOKING FOR A PLACE TO REST WHEN HE WAS STRUCK BY WILD DRIVES, NOT ONCE, BUT TWICE, AT THE 1971 U.S. OPEN. THE FIRST ZINGER CAME WHILE HALLE WAS SITTING NEAR A SHADE TREE AT THE 18TH HOLE. "*FORE ON THE RIGHT,*" WAS THE LAST THING HE HEARD BEFORE AN ERRANT DRIVE SMACKED HIM ON THE BACK. HALLE BRUSHED HIMSELF OFF AND MOVED TO ANOTHER COOL AREA, WHEN HE HEARD THE FAMILIAR WARNING—AND WAS NAILED ON THE SHOULDER!

A FIT OF ANGER COST PRO GOLFER **TOMMY BOLT** HIS FAVORITE CLUB AT THE 1960 U.S. OPEN IN DENVER. AN ENTERPRISING 10-YEAR-OLD BOY WATCHED AS THE ANGRY BOLT HEAVED HIS DRIVER INTO A LAKE. THE LAD DOVE INTO THE WATER AND EMERGED WITH CLUB IN HAND. AS THE CROWD CHEERED, BOLT THANKED THE DRIPPING WET BOY. BUT THE HAPPY YOUNGSTER DODGED THE STUNNED GOLFER AND FLED WITH THE DRIVER!

TOURING GOLFERS **WALTER HAGEN** AND **JOE KIRKWOOD** ENCOUNTERED SOME OF THE WEIRDEST COURSES DURING A GLOBAL JAUNT IN 1937. WHILE PLAYING OUTSIDE SHANGHAI, CHINA, THE MEN HAD TO CONTEND WITH SACRED BURIAL MOUNDS DOTTING THE LANDSCAPE. KIRKWOOD RECEIVED QUITE A SHOCK AFTER PLAYING HIS BALL WHEN HE LOOKED DOWN TO SEE AN ELBOW STICKING OUT FROM THE DIVOT HE'D MADE IN ONE OF THE MOUNDS!

INFAMOUS GOLF PRO **LEFTY STACKHOUSE**, WHO PLAYED IN THE LATE 1930s AND EARLY 1940s, ONCE BLEW HIS STACK AT A TOURNAMENT IN TEXAS. AFTER DRIVING SIX STRAIGHT BALLS INTO A LAKE, THE FURIOUS STACKHOUSE THREW HIS CLUB AND GOLF BAG INTO THE WATER. WHEN HIS CADDIE BEGAN TO GIGGLE, LEFTY THREW HIM IN THE DRINK, TOO. THEN, TO CAP OFF HIS WET AND WILD TIRADE, THE STEAMING DUFFER COOLED OFF BY TOSSING HIMSELF IN THE LAKE!

H. DOWIE WAS HOPPING MAD AFTER LOSING BY ONE STROKE ON THE FINAL HOLE OF A 1921 TOURNAMENT IN ONTARIO, CANADA. DOWIE THOUGHT HE WAS HEADED FOR A PLAYOFF WITH P. McGREGOR BECAUSE McGREGOR FACED A DIFFICULT BIRDIE PUTT ON THE 18TH HOLE FOR THE WIN. DOWIE WATCHED INTENTLY AS McGREGOR'S PUTT APPEARED TO STOP ON THE LIP OF THE CUP. BUT AT THE LAST MOMENT, A LARGE GRASSHOPPER LANDED SQUARELY ON THE BALL — CAUSING IT TO DROP INTO THE HOLE FOR A MIRACLE WIN!

"**CHAMPAGNE**" **TONY LEMA** BECAME SO EXCITED AFTER MAKING A DAZZLING SHOT AT THE NINTH HOLE OF THE 1957 BING CROSBY NATIONAL PRO-AM THAT HE LEAPED INTO THE AIR. PLEASURE TURNED TO PAIN, THOUGH, WHEN HE TUMBLED OVER AN 18-FOOT CLIFF AND LANDED AT THE BOTTOM. TONY SUFFERED BRUISES TO HIS SHINS, ELBOWS — AND EGO.

PRO GOLFER **PHIL RODGERS** FOUND HIMSELF OUT ON A LIMB DURING THE 1962 U.S. OPEN WHEN HIS 17TH HOLE DRIVE BECAME LODGED IN A SIX-FOOT PINE TREE. INSTEAD OF TAKING A TWO-STROKE PENALTY, RODGERS FLAILED AT THE BALL LIKE A CRAZED LUMBERJACK. IT TOOK HIM FOUR SWINGS JUST TO KNOCK THE BALL OUT OF THE TREE! PHIL WOUND UP WITH AN 8 FOR THE HOLE — AND LOST THE TOURNAMENT BY TWO STROKES.

ONE OF THE FAVORITE SCAMS OF GOLF HUSTLER **TITANIC THOMPSON** WAS BETTING HE COULD MAKE THREE OUT OF FIVE PUTTS FROM 30 FEET AWAY. WHAT HIS VICTIM DIDN'T KNOW WAS THAT THOMPSON WOULD GO OUT ON THE COURSE THE NIGHT BEFORE AND PLACE A HEAVY WATER HOSE FROM THE CUP TO THE EDGE OF THE GREEN. THIS CREATED A NEARLY INVISIBLE TROUGH WHICH THE TRICKY THOMPSON WOULD USE TO SEND HIS PUTTS EASILY INTO THE HOLE!

IN 1934, PRO GOLFER **PAUL RUNYAN** WAS THE TOP MONEY WINNER ON THE PGA CIRCUIT, PILING UP A RESPECTABLE $6,767 IN EARNINGS. UNFORTUNATELY RUNYAN'S EXPENSES FOR THE SEASON TOTALED $6,765—LEAVING POOR PAUL WITH A NET PROFIT OF $2! WELL, AT LEAST HE GOT A LOT OF FRESH AIR.

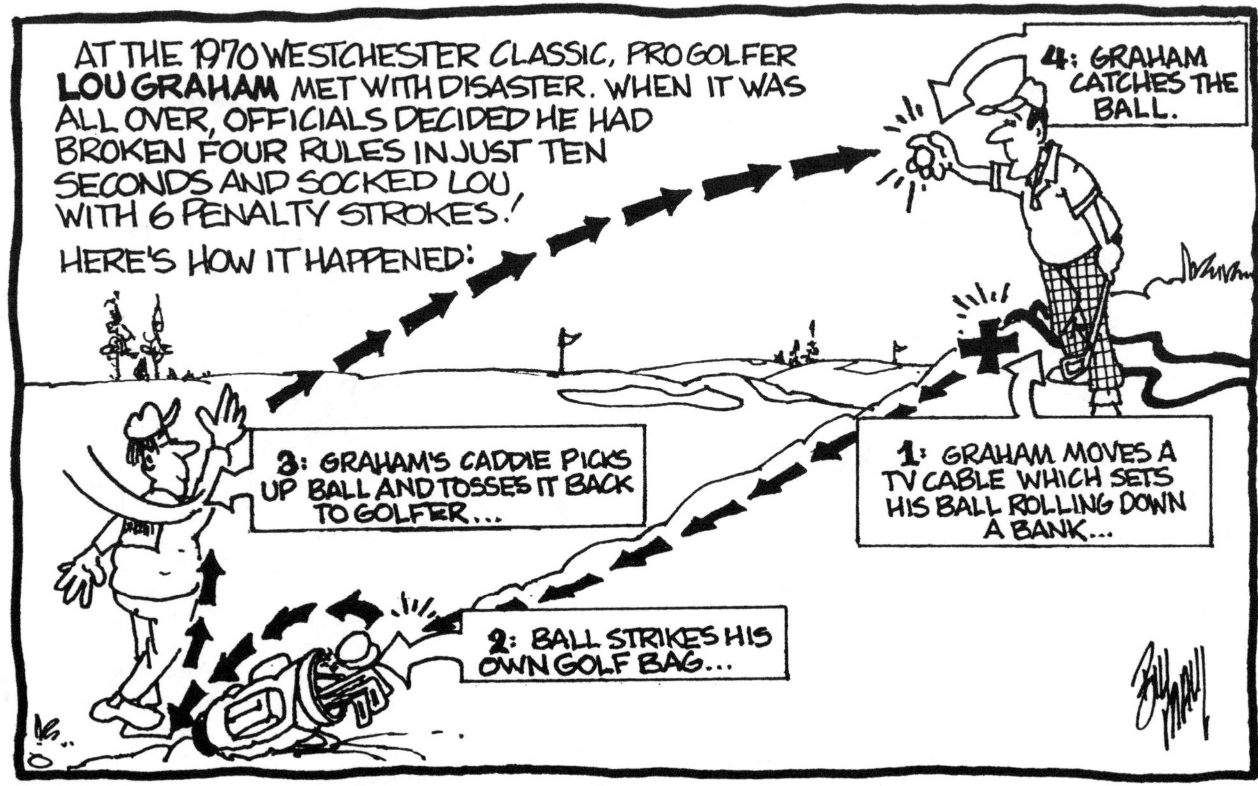
AT THE 1970 WESTCHESTER CLASSIC, PRO GOLFER LOU GRAHAM MET WITH DISASTER. WHEN IT WAS ALL OVER, OFFICIALS DECIDED HE HAD BROKEN FOUR RULES IN JUST TEN SECONDS AND SOCKED LOU WITH 6 PENALTY STROKES!
HERE'S HOW IT HAPPENED:
1: GRAHAM MOVES A TV CABLE WHICH SETS HIS BALL ROLLING DOWN A BANK...
2: BALL STRIKES HIS OWN GOLF BAG...
3: GRAHAM'S CADDIE PICKS UP BALL AND TOSSES IT BACK TO GOLFER...
4: GRAHAM CATCHES THE BALL.

18
GOLF PRO CHUCK ROTAR FELT THE EARTH MOVE AFTER HITTING A NICE APPROACH SHOT ONTO THE 18TH GREEN DURING THE 1961 ORANGE COUNTY (CALIF.) OPEN. IT WAS A MILD EARTHQUAKE. UNFORTUNATELY, THE TREMOR SHOOK HIS BALL DOWNHILL AND INTO A POND, SO ROTAR HAD TO DROP A NEW BALL AND TAKE A PENALTY STROKE. HE FINISHED WITH A DOUBLE BOGEY ON THE HOLE.

NO LINKS IN THE WORLD HAVE MORE CHAMPIONSHIP FLIGHTS THAN THE LAURENS GOLF AND COUNTRY CLUB — WHICH ALSO DOUBLES AS AN AIRPORT FOR THE SMALL IOWA TOWN. THE LOCAL AIRPORT'S SINGLE GRASS RUNWAY CUTS RIGHT THROUGH SEVEN OF THE NINE HOLES ON THE SMALL COURSE. HARDCORE DUFFERS ARE ADVISED TO LOOK RIGHT, LEFT, AND UP BEFORE TEEING OFF BECAUSE THE PLANES HAVE THE RIGHT-OF-WAY.

GOLFING BEGINNER **KAREN KNARESBOROUGH** OF NORTH HUNTINGDON, PENN., SWATTED HER TEE SHOT ON THE SIXTH HOLE OF THE MURRYSVILLE GOLF COURSE AND THEN WATCHED HER BALL GO STRAIGHT INTO THE CUP— ON THE NEARBY FIFTH GREEN. THE 1986 NOVICE TURNED TO HER HUSBAND JAMIE AND ASKED, *"IS THAT A HOLE-IN-ONE OR A MULLIGAN?"*

SPECTATORS WHO WERE TRYING TO BE HELPFUL WOUND UP HURTING THE GAME OF PRO GOLFER **DAVE MARR**. MARR'S APPROACH SHOT DURING THE 1965 BOB HOPE OPEN BOUNCED OFF THE GREEN AND ROLLED 30 FEET PAST THE HOLE— THANKS TO THE FANS WHO PARTED FROM THE BALL'S PATH. SO ON THE NEXT HOLE, THE MEMBERS OF THE GALLERY STOOD THEIR GROUND AND MARR'S SHOT STRUCK A SPECTATOR AND BOUNCED INTO A SAND TRAP!

PLAYING OUT OF A CREEK ON THE PAR FOUR 16th HOLE AT DENVER'S CHERRY HILLS COUNTRY CLUB DURING THE 1938 U.S. OPEN, PRO GOLFER **RAY AINSLEY** HACKED HIS WAY TO A RECORD 19...ON ONE HOLE! THAT'S A TRIPLE-TRIPLE-TRIPLE-TRIPLE-TRIPLE BOGEY!

PRO GOLFER **PATTI HAYES** WAS TIED FOR THE LEAD AT THE 1984 SAMARITAN TURQUOISE CLASSIC WHEN SHE BLEW AN APPROACH SHOT. INTENT ON VENTING HER ANGER, HAYES TOSSED HER SIX-IRON INTO THE AIR AND TRIED TO KICK IT ON THE WAY DOWN. HER TIMING WAS OFF AND THE CLUB HEAD BASHED HER ANKLE, CAUSING IT TO IMMEDIATELY SWELL! PATTI LIMPED THROUGH THE FINAL ROUND AND FINISHED SECOND.

AT THE 1987 TOURNAMENT PLAYERS CHAMPIONSHIP, PRO GOLFER **RAYMOND FLOYD** WHACKED A 260-YARD DRIVE SMACK DAB INTO HIS OWN GOLF BAG! FLOYD'S CADDIE HAD TAKEN A SHORT-CUT FROM THE 10TH GREEN TO THE 11TH FAIRWAY WHERE HE PLACED THE GOLF BAG ON THE EDGE OF THE ROUGH. THE BIZARRE BAG-IN-ONE COST THE ANGRY GOLFER TWO PENALTY STROKES AND THE CADDIE HIS JOB.

AMERICAN GOLFER **GENE SARAZEN** RECEIVED A LITTLE HELP IN WINNING HIS MATCH AGAINST PERCY ALLISS IN THE 1937 RYDER CUP AT SOUTHPORT, ENGLAND. SARAZEN'S APPROACH SHOT ON THE 15TH HOLE LANDED IN THE LAP OF A WOMAN, WHO PROMPTLY PICKED UP THE BALL AND TOSSED IT CLOSE TO THE HOLE! SARAZEN THEN BIRDIED THE HOLE AND WENT ON TO WIN THE MATCH.

HOUSING WAS AT A PREMIUM DURING THE 1957 BING CROSBY TOURNAMENT, SO GOLFERS **PORKY OLIVER** AND **EDDIE DARRELL** HAD TO ROOM TOGETHER. THE NEXT DAY AT THE THIRD TEE, OLIVER COMPLAINED TO HIS ROOMIE THAT HIS FEET WERE KILLING HIM. DARRELL RESPONDED THAT HIS SHOES SEEMED LOOSE. AFTER AN AWKWARD MOMENT, THE MEN REALIZED THEY WERE WEARING EACH OTHER'S SHOES AND TRADED ON THE SPOT!

WHO'S THE WORST AVID GOLFER IN THE UNITED STATES? *GOLF DIGEST* MAGAZINE ARRANGED A TOURNAMENT IN 1985 TO FIND AMERICA'S NO. 1 HACKER. **ANGELO SPAGNOLA** OF FAYETTE CITY, PA., WAS THE RUNAWAY WINNER. ON THE TPC AT SAWGRASS, ANGELO SHOT AN INCREDIBLY BAD 257 — FOR 18 HOLES! THAT'S AN AVERAGE OF MORE THAN 14 SHOTS A HOLE.

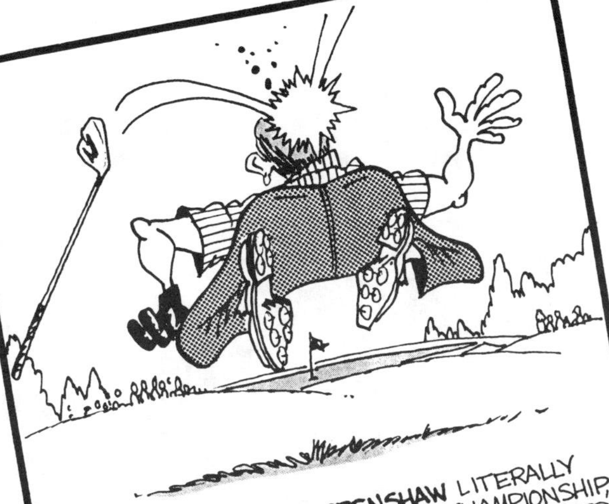

IN 1986, GOLFER **BEN CRENSHAW** LITERALLY SKULLED A SHOT. DURING THE PGA CHAMPIONSHIP, CRENSHAW TOSSED HIS CLUB INTO THE AIR AFTER HIS APPROACH SHOT ALMOST WENT INTO THE CUP ON THE 18TH HOLE. THE CLUB CAME DOWN AND HIT BEN ON THE BACK OF THE HEAD. THE EMBARRASSED GOLFER TWO-PUTTED FOR PAR AND THEN WENT TO THE HOSPITAL FOR THREE STITCHES TO CLOSE THE WOUND.

A WACKY HANDICAP MATCH AT WELLINGTON, ENGLAND, PITTED A GOLFER AGAINST A FISHERMAN USING A ROD EQUIPPED WITH A 2.5 OUNCE WEIGHT AS HIS BALL. DUFFER **RUPERT MAY** SHOT AN 87, WHILE ANGLER **J.J. MACKINLAY** NETTED A 102 IN THE 1913 CONTEST. ALTHOUGH MACKINLAY COULD CAST HIS WEIGHT UP TO 105 YARDS, HE RAN INTO TROUBLE ON SHORT CHIP SHOTS NEAR THE HOLE.

DURING HIS FIRST ROUND OF GOLF, THE LATE COMEDIAN **JIMMY DURANTE** HACKED AND FLAILED HIS WAY TO A SCORE WELL OVER 200. WHEN JIMMY ASKED HIS PLAYING PARTNERS FOLLOWING THE MARATHON MATCH, "WHAT SHALL I GIVE THE CADDIES?" ONE OF THEM SUGGESTED, "YOUR CLUBS!"

GUSTING WINDS CAUSED PRO GOLFER **J. C. SNEAD** TO BE VICTIMIZED BY AN INCREDIBLE HAT TRICK DURING THE 1977 TOURNAMENT PLAYERS CHAMPIONSHIP. SNEAD'S TRADEMARK WIDE-BRIMMED PANAMA HAT WAS BLOWN FROM HIS HEAD, AND IT ROLLED 40 YARDS DIRECTLY TOWARD THE GREEN—AND THE WIDE-EYED GOLFER'S BALL. SURE ENOUGH, THE RUNAWAY HAT NUDGED THE BALL, CAUSING OFFICIALS TO PENALIZE SNEAD TWO STROKES SINCE THE STRAW HEADGEAR WAS CONSIDERED PART OF HIS EQUIPMENT.

PLAYING THE FAMOUS ST. ANDREWS COURSE IN 1954, **HARRY LEACH** LAUNCHED THE LONGEST DRIVE IN GOLF HISTORY — WITH A LITTLE HELP. LEACH'S FIRST HOLE TEE SHOT LANDED IN THE BACK OF A RUBBISH-FILLED TRUCK THAT WAS MOTORING ALONG A ROAD NEXT TO THE FAIRWAY. THE BALL WOUND UP A MILE AWAY AT THE TOWN DUMP.

GOLFER **JENNIFER MACCURRACH** LITERALLY THREW AWAY ANY CHANCE OF FINISHING IN THE MONEY AT THE 1988 FUTURES TOURNAMENT IN BATON ROUGE, LOUISIANA. WHILE SHAKING HER BALL TO DRY IT OFF, MACCURRACH LOST HER GRIP AND SENT THE BALL FLYING INTO A WATER HAZARD! SADDLED WITH A TWO-STROKE PENALTY, JENNIFER LOST HER CONCENTRATION AND SANK IN THE STANDINGS.

IN THE FINAL ROUND OF THE 1991 PGA SUNCOAST CLASSIC IN FLORIDA, LEE TREVINO BUNGLED HIS WAY TO AN EMBARRASSING TRIPLE-BOGEY EIGHT ON THE 17TH HOLE AND LOST TO BOB CHARLES. AFTERWARD, IN EXPLAINING HIS DISASTROUS HOLE, THE UPBEAT TREVINO TOLD REPORTERS:
WELL... AT LEAST IT'S BETTER THAN A NINE!
NO. 17
GO AHEAD... MAKE MY DAY!
ELEPHANTS HAVE THE RIGHT-OF-WAY AT THE JINJA GOLF COURSE IN UGANDA, A PLACE WHICH SOMETIMES MORE CLOSELY RESEMBLES AN AFRICAN GAME PRESERVE. GUTSY GOLFERS HAVE OTHER UNSETTLING RULES TO FOLLOW. FOR INSTANCE: IF A BALL COMES TO REST IN DANGEROUS PROXIMITY TO A CROCODILE, ANOTHER BALL MAY BE DROPPED. THE SAME GOES FOR BALLS WHICH HAPPEN TO ROLL INTO HIPPOPOTAMUS FOOTPRINTS.

DURING THE 1964 BING CROSBY PRO-AM, **ARNOLD PALMER**'S TEE SHOT ON THE PAR-3 17TH HOLE LANDED IN THE SHALLOW WATER OF PEBBLE BEACH. SO ARNIE GAMELY SWUNG AWAY ON THE ROCKS AS HIS BALL BOUNCED FROM ONE ROCK TO ANOTHER. IT TOOK HIM SIX SHOTS TO GET THE BALL ONTO THE GREEN IN A 17-MINUTE DRAMA WITNESSED BY A NATIONAL TV AUDIENCE.

ONE OF THE LOCAL RULES AT **ELEPHANT HILLS CC** IN VICTORIA FALLS, ZIMBABWE, AFRICA:

IF A PLAYER'S BALL HITS A RUNNING WARTHOG, (WHICH RUNS WITH ITS TAIL POINTED STRAIGHT UP), "THIS DOES NOT ENTITLE THE PLAYER TO REPLAY THE SHOT, EXCEPT WHEN THE BALL STRIKES THE TAIL, IN WHICH CASE IT SHALL BE DEEMED TO HAVE STRUCK A MINIATURE MOVING FLAGPOLE."

AFTER BOTCHING AN EASY PUTT IN THE 1987 KEMPER OPEN, **GREG NORMAN** FELT THE URGE TO FLING HIS BALL INTO A NEARBY POND. AS GREG LET LOOSE, PLAYING PARTNER FRED COUPLES STOOD UP FROM MARKING HIS BALL. GREG'S FASTBALL SLAMMED RIGHT INTO FRED'S CHEST AND KNOCKED THE WIND OUT OF HIM! "THAT WAS MY MOST EMBARRASSING MOMENT ON THE GOLF COURSE," ADMITTED NORMAN.

BECAUSE OF HIS ARROGANCE, AMERICAN GOLFER **FRANK STRANAHAN** SO INFURIATED HIS CADDIE AT THE 1954 BRITISH AMATEUR TOURNEY THAT THE BAG-TOTER GOT EVEN. WITH A HIGH RIDGE SHIELDING STRANAHAN FROM THE HOLE, HE ORDERED HIS CADDIE TO LINE HIM UP WITH THE PIN. SO THE CADDIE MOVED TO A SPOT AND TOLD THE GOLFER TO SHOOT OVER HIM. STRANAHAN'S SHOT THEN FLEW DIRECTLY OVER THE CADDIE—AND INTO A THICK PATCH OF WAIST-HIGH FERNS WHERE IT WAS LOST FOR GOOD!

IN THE 1950 U.S. OPEN, GOLFER **LLOYD MANGRUM** WAS ABOUT TO PUTT ON THE 16TH HOLE OF A PLAYOFF WHEN HE NOTICED A GNAT RESTING ON HIS **BALL**. HE PICKED UP THE BALL, BLEW THE GNAT AWAY, AND THEN PUTTED FOR PAR. ONLY THEN DID HE FIND OUT IT WAS A TWO-STROKE PENALTY FOR LIFTING A BALL IN PLAY. IT COST MANGRUM THE PLAYOFF.

DURING THE 1912 AMATEUR CHAMPIONSHIP IN ENGLAND, **ABE MITCHELL** WAS LEADING BY TWO STROKES IN THE RAIN IN THE FINAL ROUND. BUT MITCHELL'S TEE SHOT ON THE 14TH HOLE RICOCHETED OFF AN OPEN UMBRELLA NEAR THE GREEN AND BOUNCED INTO A BUNKER. HIS GAME TURNED ALL WET AS HE LOST THE HOLE AND EVENTUALLY THE TOURNAMENT TO JOHN BALL.

PRO GOLFER **PAYNE STEWART** HAD THE PANTS BEATEN OFF HIM AFTER MAKING A WACKY WAGER DURING THE 1988 LEUKEMIA CLASSIC EXHIBITION MATCH IN WILMINGTON, DEL. PLAYING AGAINST A TRIO OF TOP WOMEN GOLFERS, STEWART BET HE'D BEAT THEIR BEST SCORE PER HOLE — WITH THE LOSER DOFFING THEIR PANTS. THE WOMEN ROSE TO THE CHALLENGE BY BEATING STEWART WHO PROMPTLY REMOVED HIS FAMOUS KNICKERS TO THE DELIGHT OF THE GALLERY.

PORT
'O
LET
PRO FOOTBALL QUARTERBACK **JIM McMAHON**
PROVIDED SOME UNPLANNED BATHROOM HUMOR
WHEN HE WAS CAUGHT WITH HIS PANTS DOWN
DURING A 1989 CELEBRITY GOLF TOURNAMENT.
THE PARTICIPANTS WORE LIVE MICROPHONES
AT THE PRO-CELEBRITY SKINS GAME IN SUB-
URBAN CHICAGO. THE GALLERY WAS TREATED
TO STRANGE SOUNDS AND OFF-COLOR REMARKS
WHEN THE MIKED McMAHON VISITED THE REST-
ROOM IN THE MIDDLE OF HIS GOLF GAME!

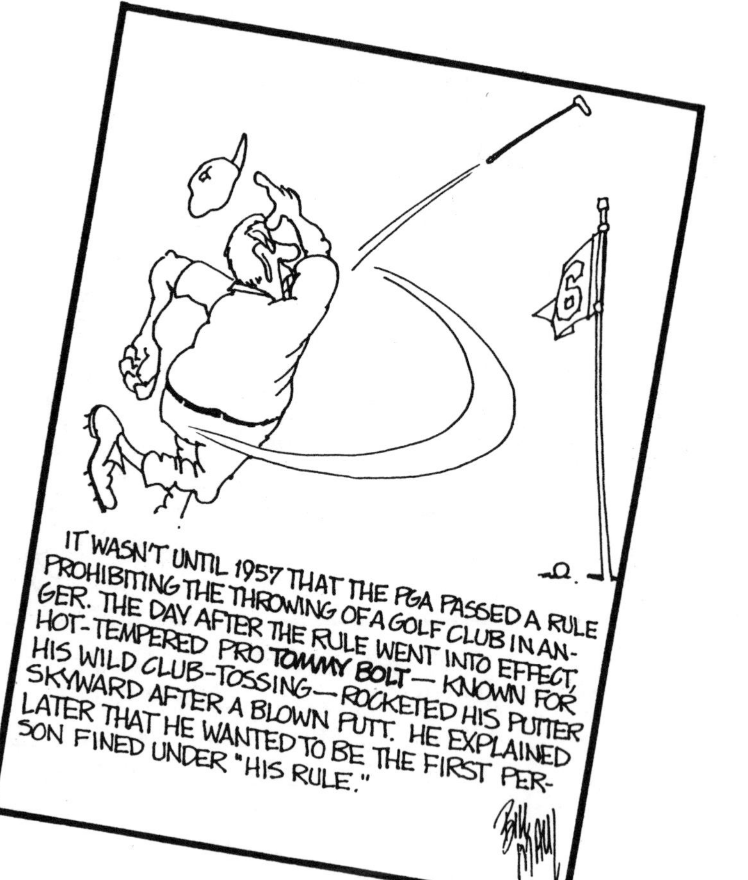
6
IT WASN'T UNTIL 1957 THAT THE PGA PASSED A RULE
PROHIBITING THE THROWING OF A GOLF CLUB IN AN-
GER. THE DAY AFTER THE RULE WENT INTO EFFECT,
HOT-TEMPERED PRO **TOMMY BOLT**— KNOWN FOR
HIS WILD CLUB-TOSSING— ROCKETED HIS PUTTER
SKYWARD AFTER A BLOWN PUTT. HE EXPLAINED
LATER THAT HE WANTED TO BE THE FIRST PER-
SON FINED UNDER "HIS RULE."

IN THE 1969 U.S. OPEN, **BOB ROSBURG** ONLY NEEDED TO TAP IN AN EASY THREE-FOOT PUTT ON THE FINAL HOLE TO GET INTO A PLAYOFF. INCREDIBLY, ROSBURG BLEW THE SHOT TO SET THE DUBIOUS RECORD FOR THE SHORTEST MISSED PUTT ON THE 72ND HOLE TO LOSE THE U.S. OPEN BY ONE STROKE.

AUSTRALIAN GOLF PRO **BRUCE DEVLIN** CAN BOAST OF HAVING A WATER HAZARD NAMED AFTER HIM—BUT HE PROBABLY WON'T. ONLY TWO STROKES BEHIND THE LEADER ON THE FINAL HOLE OF THE 1975 SAN DIEGO OPEN, DEVLIN NEEDED AN EAGLE ON THE PAR-5 TO TIE FOR THE LEAD. BUT HIS SECOND SHOT LANDED IN A POND. IT TOOK HIM SEVEN STROKES TO BLAST OUT OF THE WATER AS HE PLUNGED TO 30TH PLACE. THE HAZARD THUS BECAME KNOWN AS "DEVLIN'S BILLABONG"—AUSTRALIAN FOR POND.

PRO GOLFER KY LAFFOON TREATED HIS CLUBS AS IF THEY WERE HIS ARCH ENEMIES. ONCE, AFTER HITTING A POOR PUTT AT THE 1947 JACKSONVILLE OPEN, LAFFOON SHOCKED THE GALLERY BY TRYING TO "KILL" HIS PUTTER. SQUEEZING THE NECK OF THE SHAFT, LAFFOON WADED ANKLE-DEEP INTO A CREEK, SHOVED HIS CLUB UNDER THE WATER, AND SCREAMED:
DROWN, YOU @★!!@★!, DROWN!

AT THE 1973 SEA PINES HERITAGE CLASSIC, PRO GOLFER **HALE IRWIN** AGREED TO A SLIGHT CHANGE IN THE RULES WHEN HIS ERRANT DRIVE WOUND UP INSIDE THE BRA OF A SURPRISED SPECTATOR. THE RED-FACED WOMAN SAID THE BALL STRUCK HER IN THE CHEST BEFORE FLOPPING INSIDE HER UNDERGARMENT. THE COURSE RULE CALLING FOR THE GOLFER TO REMOVE THE BALL FROM ITS OBSTRUCTION WAS WAIVED AND HALE GRANTED THE HONORS TO THE WOMAN.

ZIP!

GOLFING GREAT **SAM SNEAD** SAW HIS CHANCES FOR A WIN AT THE CLEVELAND OPEN GO DOWN THE TOILET WHEN HIS APPROACH SHOT ON THE 18TH HOLE TOOK OFF TOWARD THE LOCKER ROOM. JUST AS THE BALL WAS ABOUT TO CAROM OFF THE BUILDING, A POLICE OFFICER OPENED THE DOOR. SAM'S BALL WHIZZED PAST THE COP'S EAR AND ENDED UP IN THE LAST STALL OF THE MEN'S TOILET! THE 2-SHOT PENALTY COST SNEAD FIRST PLACE BY ONE STROKE.

THE UNOFFICIAL RECORD FOR THE LONGEST PUTT IN GOLF HISTORY BELONGS TO **DALE DOUGLASS** WHO WAS FORCED TO TEE OFF THE FIRST ROUND OF THE 1981 KEMPER OPEN WITH HIS PUTTER. BECAUSE OF A MIX-UP, HIS CADDIE AND CLUBS WERE AT THE WRONG TEE. SO, DOUGLASS USED HIS PUTTER TO STROKE THE BALL 150 YARDS STRAIGHT DOWN THE FAIRWAY! THE RED-FACED CADDIE CAUGHT UP IN TIME FOR DALE'S SECOND SHOT AT THE CONGRESSIONAL COUNTRY CLUB IN BETHESDA, MD.

AN ATTEMPT BY GOLFERS TO SHAME A "TORTOISE" INTO SPEEDING UP HIS PLAY FAILED MISERABLY AT THE 1922 SCOTTISH AMATEUR CHAMPIONSHIP. COMPETITORS BROUGHT A FULL-SIZED BED TO THE COURSE AND LOUNGED ON IT WHILE THE DEPLORABLY SLOW PLAYER, **ROBERT WELLS**, SIZED UP HIS SHOTS. THE COMPETITORS GOT PLENTY OF REST, BECAUSE THE SLOWPOKE PLAYED EVEN MORE DELIBERATELY IN THE FINAL ROUND.

PRO GOLFER **GARY PLAYER** WAS PUSHED INTO A LAKE BY ADORING FANS AT THE 1964 U.S. OPEN. GARY HAD JUST FINISHED A PRACTICE ROUND AND WAS SIGNING AUTOGRAPHS FOR THE OVER-EAGER CROWD. THE FANS KEPT BACKING HIM UP UNTIL HE FELL INTO THE WATER. THE DRENCHED PLAYER KEPT HIS COOL, STOOD UP IN THE SHALLOW WATER, AND CONTINUED TO SIGN AUTOGRAPHS FOR HIS FANS.

AN INNOCENT-LOOKING ACORN COST GOLFER **BEN CRENSHAW** HIS 1987 RYDER CUP MATCH AGAINST SCOTLAND'S EAMONN DARCY, ONE OF THE WEAKER PLAYERS ON THE EUROPEAN TEAM. STANDING OFF THE GREEN AND WAITING TO PUTT, BEN CASUALLY TAPPED THE ACORN WITH HIS PUTTER—AND WATCHED THE CLUB'S SHAFT SNAP! CRENSHAW HAD TO USE HIS 1-IRON TO PUTT ON THE BACK NINE AND DIDN'T FARE TOO WELL. AS A RESULT, HE LOST TO DARCY.

TEXAS GOLF PRO **HENRY RANSOM** QUIT IN ANGER AFTER RUNNING INTO TROUBLE AT CYPRESS POINT'S INFAMOUS 16TH HOLE. RANSOM'S TEE SHOT HIT A CLIFF BELOW THE GREEN AND FELL TO THE BEACH. AFTER THREE FAILED WEDGE SHOTS, HIS FOURTH ATTEMPT RICOCHETED OFF THE ROCKY CLIFF AND STRUCK HIM SQUARE IN THE MID-SECTION. THE FRUSTRATED GOLFER PICKED UP HIS CLUBS AND LEFT THE COURSE REMARKING: *"WHEN THE HOLE STARTS HITTING BACK AT ME, IT'S TIME TO QUIT!"*

**LEFTY STACKHOUSE** WAS A RAGING INFERNO WHO TURNED GOLF INTO A CONTACT SPORT DURING THE LATE 1930s AND EARLY '40s BY INFLICTING PAIN ON HIMSELF WHENEVER THINGS WENT WRONG. ONCE, HE PUNCHED HIMSELF IN THE JAW WITH A VICIOUS UPPERCUT AFTER MISSING A SHORT PUTT. STUNNED OBSERVERS WATCHED AS STACKHOUSE FELL TO HIS KNEES — AND THEN KNOCKED HIMSELF OUT WITH A SECOND PUNCH TO THE CHOPS!

SUPERSTAR GOLFERS **JACK NICKLAUS** AND **GARY PLAYER** HAD TO SKIP ONE HOLE OF THEIR $50,000 CHALLENGE SERIES IN 1966 DUE TO SWARMING BEES ON THE COURSE. NICKLAUS AND PLAYER FOLLOWED A SPECTATOR'S SUGGESTION OF SMEARING MUD ON THEIR FACES, BUT THE GOLFERS ONLY ENDED UP DIRTY AND STUNG BEFORE FLEEING TO THE NEXT HOLE.

DARKNESS WAS SETTLING OVER THE COURSE IN MUS-SELBURGH, SCOTLAND, WHEN **ROBERT CLARK** GRUDGINGLY AGREED TO CALL OFF THE SEARCH FOR HIS BALL ON THE 18TH HOLE. MOMENTS LATER, THE BALL TURNED UP WHERE IT HAD BEEN ALL ALONG— IN THE CUP! CLARK WOULD HAVE WON THE 1870 MATCH IF HE HAD FOUND HIS HOLE-IN-ONE BEFORE CALLING IT QUITS.